A Dream of Maya

ⵎ ⵎ ⵎ

*Panorama with the Nunnery
Quadrangle on the left and
Adivino Pyramid on the right,
Uxmal, circa 1873. Le Plongeon shot the panorama from
the Governor's Palace using
two overlapping 5 × 8 inch
photographs.*

A Dream of Maya

Augustus and Alice Le Plongeon
in Nineteenth-Century Yucatan

Lawrence Gustave Desmond
Phyllis Mauch Messenger

Foreword by Jaime Litvak King

University of New Mexico Press
Albuquerque

Cover photo—A composite photo by Augustus Le Plongeon. The eight reed bas-relief, Alice preparing to mount her horse, and Augustus in his field clothing were photographed at Chichen Itza and later put together to form a single photo in his laboratory. The photos were taken around 1883, but the date of the laboratory work is unknown. Original negatives and prints are lost.

Library of Congress Cataloging-in-Publication Data

Desmond, Lawrence Gustave, 1935–
  A dream of Maya.

  Bibliography: p.
  Includes index.
  1. Le Plongeon, Augustus, 1826–1908. 2. Le Plongeon, Alice, d. 1910.
3. Mayas—Antiquities. 4. Archaeologists—Biography. 5. Photographers—
Biography. 6. Indians of Mexico—Yucatán (State)—Antiquities. 7. Yucatán
(Mexico : State)—Antiquities. 8. Mexico—Antiquities. I. Messenger, Phyllis
Mauch, 1950–   II. Title.
F1435.L4D47   1987   972′.6501   87-19122
ISBN 0-8263-1000-1 (pbk.)

Credits: Unless otherwise indicated photographs are by Augustus Le Plongeon and are used courtesy of the Philosophical Research Society, Los Angeles, California.
Design: Barbara Jellow

Contents

Illustrations

To my parents,
Lawrence C. Desmond
and
Gritli Desmond-Mueller,
who were loving and understanding.

To D.E.P. and to Skip and Lindsay Carmen Messenger,
who were all part of the process.

Foreword

I was about thirteen when I first read Augustus Le Plongeon's *Queen Móo and the Egyptian Sphinx*. I found it in the Benjamin Franklin Library in Mexico City. At the time, I was reading everything I could get my hands on that dealt with archaeology and, since the book was in the section that contained books on ancient Egypt, I took it home and read it. It impressed me quite a bit. For one thing it didn't deal with Egypt but with something closer to home—the Maya. For another it spoke of links between the New World and the Old. Not in vague terms but in a very precise and concrete way. Ruling families, domains, travels, and statues. It also suggested a number of words that, according to the author, proved that the ancient Egyptians were connected to the Maya.

I must have been an inquisitive kid then. I was certainly stubborn for I tried to follow Le Plongeon's train of thought.

I plagued my history teacher with questions and tried to read other books on the subject. There weren't many. My teacher said that Le Plongeon was wrong, that the writer hadn't taken into account that the Maya and the Egyptians lived at very different times. He was right, of course, and when I corroborated it I stopped that line of inquiry.

Many years later, as a student of archaeology, I heard the rumor from others that Le Plongeon had used explosives for digging. We, of course, had just been through Mortimer Wheeler's *Archaeology from the Earth* and had been converted to careful digging, so the old Mayanist was pretty much the epitome of everything we wanted to avoid. I was also able to read Robert Wauchope's *Lost Tribes and Sunken Continents*. Le Plongeon was mentioned there, his life told, his assertions questioned, and his theories and ideas dissected and revealed to be nonsense. Wauchope had written his book in a very angry mood and it clearly showed that non-scientific archaeology was not only wrong but also very damaging. He was right, of course.

A few years later I met Larry Desmond. He was starting his research for this book and was falling in love with Le Plongeon. My initial reaction was that Desmond was showing signs of brainwashing. What was there to write about the old geezer? He was a lousy digger and he was wildly wrong in his crazy theories. Why so much work?

In time I understood why. It didn't have anything to do with his ideas, flaky as some of them might have been, or with the quality of his excavations. It had everything to do with the type of activity that archaeology was in Le Plongeon's time and how the general public conceived—and still does to a very high degree—the work of exploring and excavating sites.

Athena, the Greek goddess of wisdom, was born, large and wise, out of her father Zeus's head. It is a bad allegory. Sciences are never born full-grown. They develop out of lore that is later seen as non-scientific. The first researchers in a given field make assertions that future generations consider nonsense. Aristotle's work is a good example. Science is not fully developed in his writings but its origins are there. After a time those ideas are questioned and other theories, many times as nonsensical as the former ones, are advanced in their place. Both cases are probably the normal result of insufficient, unsystematically collected evidence. It is only when enough data has been collected, when an ongoing discussion of theory and facts has proceeded for some time, and when the field has developed a methodology for gathering, understanding, and explaining the parts of reality that constitute its scope that modern science, universalist and generalist, can be recognized as such.

In this scheme Le Plongeon clearly belongs to the second phase as do the theory of phlogiston in chemistry, Lamarck's theory of heredity of acquired traits in biology, Flammarion's catastrophism in astronomy, or the work of Franz Joseph Gall and Johann Spurzheim in psychology that developed into phrenology. None of these theories is accepted by modern science but the lives, ideas, and the work that led to them is important for the history of science. This book deals with such a time. Archaeology was contending, as seriously as it could, with the data it had and the body of theory it could develop, attempting to find explanations that made sense. If what was done then doesn't look good now, it wasn't only Le Plongeon at fault. Consider what was being said and done by people like Schliemann or Brasseur. And don't forget what profession swallowed Piltdown whole some years later.

The history of archaeology as a field has become quite important and some books, such as Willey and Sabloff's *A History of American Archaeology,* are important compendia. The book on Le Plongeon does not follow that generalistic trend. It concentrates on one character and proceeds on the assumption (correct as far as I am concerned) that his life is relevant to the understanding of his work. Since he was influential in the development of Maya archaeology, it helps in understanding why it is as it is and why it became so. As such it is a significant contribution both for the general history of archaeology and for Maya research.

Every profession projects a stereotype. For the public mind the chemist is a man in a dirty, acid-specked lab coat who holds some container full of a foul-smelling liquid up to the light. An entomologist runs around with a butterfly net. A physicist is an absent-minded being who forgets things. Indiana Jones is the archaeologist.

There is a difference between those stereotypes. Ours is not fiction. Some of the first archaeologists faced dangers no less than the ones Indy went through. Angry natives, savage beasts, and wild country really existed and it was people like Le Plongeon who had to be there to dig. And dig they did, as well as they knew how. Le Plongeon is one of the causes for the stereotype of the archaeologist even today. Romantic adventurer, garrulous adversary, a character out of a Jules Verne novel, Le Plongeon was bigger than life in his time and today, when the world is quite a bit blander, a reminder that things weren't always so. Le Plongeon's life brings us to the reasons for public interest in archaeology.

This book accomplishes its authors' purpose, to synthesize the life of one of the most notable archaeologist-travelers of the end of the nineteenth century and to let the reader in on a number of previously unknown details of his life. Le Plongeon was controversial, even in his time, both for his ideas and for his methods. His wife has never been regarded before as more than just her husband's loyal helper. This book makes important points and provides a new perspective on both its subjects.

Desmond and Messenger have researched their topic well. They have quoted from contemporary papers, have paid attention to American and Mexican scholarly opinion of the time, and have shown due regard for the Yucatec sources. *A Dream of Maya* is not only a scholarly book. It is a very entertaining read. The authors, wisely, have not attempted to enter into a deep analysis of Le Plongeon's work. Such a task would be irrelevant now. Le Plongeon is "history" and should be looked upon as such. He deserves a biography and Desmond and Messenger have given him a very nice one, as good as any other one on the ancestors of modern archaeology—or of Indiana Jones. They are quite plainly sympathetic to their subject, and being conscious of it, they have been careful. The resulting work is well rounded, well written, well revised, and damned interesting. I have enjoyed writing this foreword. Maybe the old geezer was telling us something he didn't say explicitly after all.

Jaime Litvak King
Cholula, Puebla, Mexico

April, 1987

Preface

If Augustus Le Plongeon had been given a fair shake by historians of anthropology or history, this book might never have been written. It was the unusual vehemence of the attacks on his work and a fascination with this unique nineteenth-century character that led to a search of archives and photo collections by Larry Desmond in 1977. Desmond's goal was to try to explain why such an absurd-sounding character as Le Plongeon was so intriguing. One of the missing pieces that fell into place was a major collection of the "Old Doctor's" glass-plate negatives and original albumen prints. With that discovery Desmond knew he was hooked. Desmond's research on Augustus Le Plongeon led him to archives around the country, to fieldwork in Yucatan, and to a Ph.D. dissertation.

When Luther Wilson and Beth Hadas of the University of New Mexico Press suggested that Larry and I work together on Le Plongeon's biography, we wondered why we hadn't considered the idea ourselves. I had been following Larry's progress from the beginning, when he pounded out a draft of his research notes in the basement of our house in Deephaven, Minnesota, but it had not occurred to me to join him full time on the project.

The picture that took shape from Augustus and Alice Le Plongeon's ethnographic writing, photographs, field-notes, and drawings was of an extraordinary couple whose work was not being fairly appraised in the context of the time and situation. We soon found that Alice's role, and the roles Alice and Augustus played in each other's lives were becoming clearer. Their personalities and their part in that period of discovery and exploration began to emerge as we pieced together the sequence of events and let the Le Plongeons speak in their own eloquent voices as much as possible.

For the Le Plongeons, their research was their life, and their psyches were intertwined with their work. They never had children. In a way, the Maya were the Le Plongeons' family and they were as unable to see their imperfections as parents would be. Alice and Augustus could never reconcile themselves to the lack of acceptance their efforts achieved.

I hope that we have succeeded in helping them live again.

Phyllis Mauch Messenger

Note: Accents have been used for titles and names but not for place-names.

Some photographs originally shot in stereo by Le Plongeon are reproduced directly from his negatives to illustrate the overlapping double image needed for stereo viewing. However, no adjustment of size or positioning has been made to actually create stereo imaging.

Acknowledgments

Many people have given me assistance and encouragement during the research for this book. It is the sum of their contributions that has made this project possible.

Manly P. Hall, president and founder of the Philosophical Research Society, encouraged this work, and generously allowed me to work with and print the Le Plongeon glass negatives. His staff, including librarian Pearl Thomas and assistant Edith Waldron, were always ready to locate obscure articles and materials in the Society's collections.

Other assistance with Le Plongeon's photographs came from Ansel Adams, Pirkle Jones at the San Francisco Art Institute, Richard F. Carter, Ralph E. Black, and Larry Harwood of the University of Colorado.

At a crucial moment early in my work on Augustus Le Plongeon, Linnea Wren had the good sense to steer me into Gordon Willey's office. He encouraged me to continue, and expand my research perspective since he felt Le Plongeon's work deserved a closer look.

Later, at the University of Colorado, Russ McGoodwin reviewed my years of work on Le Plongeon and helped me bring that research to fruition as a Ph.D. dissertation.

Fieldwork in Yucatan was facilitated by archaeologists Norberto Gonzales C., and Peter Schmidt of the Instituto Nacional de Antropología e Historia, and by Susan Milbrath of the Florida State Museum.

A number of institutions and individuals were of great help with archival research. Sincere thanks to Sally L. Bond, Ian Graham, and Daniel W. Jones, Jr., of the Peabody Museum of Archaeology and Ethnology, Harvard University; Gordon F. Ekholm, American Museum of Natural History; M. J. De La Haye of the Société Jersiaise; William Joyce, American Antiquarian Society; Thomas Niehaus, Latin American Library of Tulane University; Franklin Portugal, Carnegie Institution of Washington; Diane Trubandt, John Q. Packard Library in Marysville, California; the staffs of the Albany Institute of History and Art in New York, Bancroft Library of the University of California in Berkeley, the Bibliothèque Nationale in Paris, the Brooklyn Museum, California Academy of Sciences in San Francisco, l'Ecole Polytechnique of Paris, the Long Island Historical Society, the Metropolitan Museum of Art, the Mormon Church's Genealogical Library, Musée de l'Homme in Paris, and the Smithsonian Institution.

Many individuals assisted by providing information, encouragement, or comments. Their invaluable help is gratefully acknowledged. They include George Andrews, Anthony Aveni, Elizabeth Baquedano, Cara Billot, Jacques Barchilon, Davíd Carrasco, David and Vilma Casares, Curtis M. Hinsley, Jr., A. F. C. Jackson, A. A. Keim, Jaime Litvak King, Shirley W. Lee, Frank Le Maistre, Keith McElroy, Paula McFarland, Barbara McLeod, Susan Milbrath, A. E. Mourant, H. B. Nicholson, Donald Patterson, Ross Parmenter, Dorie Reents, Linda Schele, George Stuart, John Weeks, Clarence and Marian Weiant, Shelley Vaughan Williams, and David and Linnea Wren.

The support and interest of the staff at the University of New Mexico Press has been extremely important. Former director Luther Wilson, director Beth Hadas, and editor Claire Sanderson have all played a vital role.

Archaeologist Skip Messenger, who patiently put up with the "Old Doctor's" long intrusion into his household, lent his artistic skills by rendering maps and drawings from the Le Plongeons' mural tracings which are an important contribution to the aesthetics of this book.

Introduction

False facts are highly injurious to the progress of science, for they often long endure; but false views, if supported by some evidence, do little harm, as every one takes a salutary pleasure in proving their falseness; and when this is done, one path towards error is closed, and the truth is often at the same time opened.
—*Charles Darwin,* The Descent of Man, *1871*

Augustus and Alice Dixon Le Plongeon entered American archaeology at a critical juncture in its development. Archaeology was developing as an academic discipline, moving from speculation to description and gathering of facts. By the last quarter of the century the self-trained archaeologists were being replaced by university-trained professionals.

As early as the 1840s, influential men in the field, such as Joseph Henry of the Smithsonian Institution, admonished researchers not to speculate on precolumbian civilization, but to wait until all the facts were in. In his 1857 *Observations on Mexican History and Archaeology*, Branz Mayer wrote,

> The American antiquarian should, as yet, avoid the
> peril of starting in his investigations with an
> hypothesis, for the chances are very great that, in

the mythic confusion of our aboriginal past, he will
find abundant hints to justify any ideas excited by
his credulity and hopes. In the present state of
archaeology, all labors should be contributions to
that store of facts, which, in time, may form a mass
of testimony.

Several early researchers and explorers were key figures
in the early development of Maya research.

Jean Frédérick Waldeck, who worked in the Maya area
in the 1830s, documented the ruined cities on the Yucatan
peninsula by illustrating hundreds of structures and motifs.
He was later criticized as being too interpretive in a number
of his drawings, as well as for proposing Asiatic origins for
the Maya.

Following more closely the dictates of the times, John
Lloyd Stephens and Frederick Catherwood achieved great
success in producing beautifully illustrated books of their
travels in Yucatan and Central America. They knew the value
of photographs in documentation and attempted to use the
daguerreotype photographic process, but found it difficult
to use in the field. Catherwood finally resorted to the *camera
lucida,* a well-proven method that allowed the illustrator to
trace the image directly onto paper. His color drawings were
an impressive and important step in the documentation of
the archaeological sites, but they lacked the detail of a photograph and were often romantic in style. Their purpose was
not only to record but also to impress the viewer. And their
text conformed to the admonishments of men like Henry,
avoiding almost all speculation or interpretation.

During the second quarter of the nineteenth century
the scholar Brasseur de Bourbourg spent a number of years
in the Maya region. As a result of that fieldwork he wrote
the four-volume *Histoire des nations civilisées du Mexique et
de l'Amérique centrale* in 1856. At the time of its publication
it was well received by scholars, albeit reluctantly, because
its conclusions were based on limited factual knowledge.
Later he published his *Quatre lettres sur le Mexique,* and was
severely condemned as being overly speculative in promot-
ing the hypothesis that America was the mother continent
of world civilization.

In the 1860s Désiré Charnay, a French photographer,
documented several Maya ruins using the new glass-plate
negative process that had been developed a decade earlier.
His work produced the first successful and widely known
photographs of these structures. While the quality of his
photographic work was excellent, his short stays at the various sites limited the number of photographs he took and

prevented systematic recording. His intent was to provide views of the ruins, rather than an in-depth documentary record of the sites.

While Charnay's writings fell within the bounds of description, he did attempt to provide some interpretation. It consisted mainly of comparing Mesoamerican cultures with the civilizations of Asia, and identifying the Toltecs of Highland Mexico as the civilizers of Mesoamerica—a theory that has never found any support.

In 1873 the Le Plongeons landed in Yucatan prepared to document the ruins by the same new photographic method Charnay had used and by making architectural plans and drawings. Augustus felt well prepared for what he saw as his life's work. He brought years of experience in surveying and photography, most recently in Peru, and he, unlike his predecessors, brought with him a hypothesis to be tested by systematic observation. He openly stated that he came to Yucatan with the hypothesis that the Maya were the founders of world civilization. He would let the facts either prove or disprove that hypothesis.

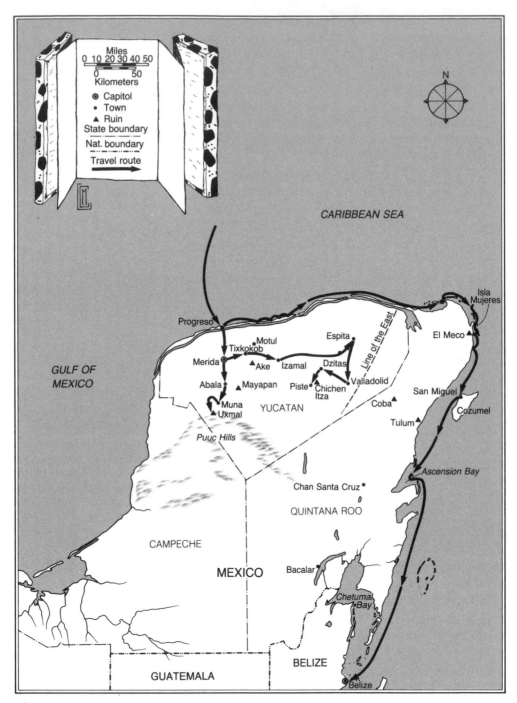

The Yucatan Peninsula in the 1870s

Map shows sites and towns visited by Alice and Augustus Le Plongeon during their eleven years of fieldwork. Route arrows show 1) arrival in Merida from Cuba, 2) Merida to Uxmal, 3) Merida to Chichen Itza, and 4) voyage from Progreso to Belize. This map has been adapted by Bill Nelson from a map originally drawn by Lewis C. Messenger, Jr.

Chapter 1

Charting a Course

We are pleased to learn that our friend Plongeon, who has his Gallery of Daguerritypes [sic] . . . has been obliged to employ additional assistants as a consequence of a rush of business.—
San Francisco Daily Evening Bulletin, *October 20, 1855*

If Alice Dixon Le Plongeon had one disappointment about the thirty-seven years with her husband, it was that Augustus had died so misunderstood and maligned by his contemporaries. Their years of exploration and research together in Yucatan had produced volumes of text and hundreds of photographs, yet it seemed that most archaeologists and Maya scholars in established positions were against them.

When Augustus Le Plongeon died in 1908 at the age of eighty-two, it was his belief in ancient Maya civilization as the mother culture of the world that stood out in people's minds. His pioneering excavations, architectural floor plans and cross-sections, and detailed photographic records, carried out during a period of indigenous uprisings in Yucatan, were largely forgotten, as were his earlier achievements in medicine and the natural sciences.

For her part Alice's narratives of life in the wilds, analyses of Maya history after the Spanish conquest, and epic metaphysical poems about Maya princes and queens were widely published. Alice's writing was as prolific as Augustus's, and obviously the more literary of the two. Nonetheless, many perceived Alice as a mere wife following after her husband, echoing his thoughts.

Widowed at the age of fifty-seven, without having reaped financial rewards from their discoveries, Alice did the only thing she could. She continued to write feverishly, hoping to finish their work before she, too, died. Yellow fever and malaria had taken their toll from the day she first set foot in Yucatan as a young bride, led from England by the determined Frenchman who had already seen so much of the world. While she still was able, Alice was determined to do what she could to alter the undeserved reputation of her husband's work.

In a tribute to Augustus Le Plongeon published in 1909 by the International Congress of Americanists, Alice emphasized his character and the roots of his motivation. "This active traveller and ardent scholar never consented to write a word about his own life, but always maintained that a man's work was the only important thing for his fellow-beings." In this case, she concluded, his work alone was not enough, so she filled in details of his family background, education, and early experiences that she hoped would bolster the tarnished image of her husband.

Augustus Henry Julius Le Plongeon was born May 4, 1826 to French parents on the Island of Jersey, one of the Channel Islands off the northwest coast of France. According to Alice, his father, François Guillaume Le Plongeon, was a member of the Legion of Honor, and a commodore in the French navy; his mother, Frances, was the daughter of Le Gros du Roche, governor of Mont Saint-Michele. His great uncle was Lord Jersey. His was an auspicious beginning.

Augustus entered the military college at Caen when he was eleven. While there he learned of his mother's death, a devastating blow to the young boy. Her "memory remained ever sacred to him," Alice wrote in her tribute to Augustus. In 1841 Augustus began his schooling at the École Polytechnique in Paris and at age nineteen graduated with full honors.

After graduation Augustus and a friend purchased a yacht and set sail for South America, hoping to travel and see the sights in that exotic land. Their boat was wrecked just off the coast of Chile. Somehow the two companions managed to swim ashore and made their way to the coastal town of Valparaiso. Augustus decided to settle in Chile for

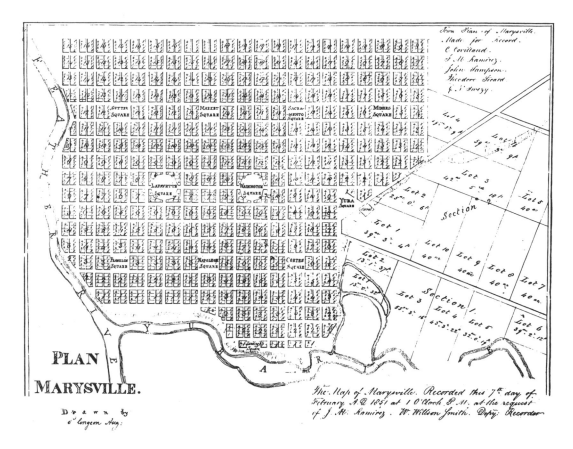

Drawn by
e' longeon Aug:

Augustus Le Plongeon's plan of Marysville, California recorded February 7, 1851. For surveying and mapping the town, Le Plongeon received five choice lots near Landing Square, on the banks of the Yuba River. Courtesy of John Packard Library, Marysville, CA.

a time and found work teaching in a local college. Reflecting the broad and general educational preparation of the time, he taught drawing, mathematics, and languages.

When news of the California gold rush reached Valparaiso Le Plongeon decided to sail to San Francisco. Again, formidable storms during the voyage nearly cost him his life. But the ship was spared and reached the California coast, where Augustus soon found another use for his navigational skills.

In 1850 he filed his professional card with the *Marysville Herald,* offering his services as surveyor and engineer. He was hired to lay out the streets of Marysville, using a ship's quadrant. The town lay at the confluence of the Yuba and Feather rivers, a potentially important spot for river commerce. Le Plongeon's signed and dated plan of the town was accepted by the city fathers in February 1851. He was also requested to provide a survey and plan for Linda, another town being established nearby.

As payment for his services as surveyor and city planner, Le Plongeon was given the deeds to about twelve plots of land in those infant goldrush towns. From a set of five choice lots near Landing Square in Marysville, he sold several twenty-foot frontages and some larger pieces, making a profit of $30,000. Le Plongeon carefully set aside this and other payments he received as a land agent to finance future travels to South America.

Another key figure in the establishment of Marysville was Stephen J. Field, who like so many others hearing of the California gold rush came with little money but great enthusiasm. Within three weeks of arriving with only ten dollars to his name, he purchased sixty-five lots for over $16,000, and had been elected Marysville's chief civil magistrate. For several years Field and Le Plongeon worked in tandem on land transactions, becoming close friends. Field went on to become a justice of the United States Supreme Court with power enough to influence the President of Mexico when Le Plongeon called on his old friend thirty years later.

In 1851 Augustus went to Europe while recuperating from a serious illness. His travels took him to the Great Exhibition at Sydenham Palace in England. There Augustus was quite taken by a demonstration of a new photographic technique using paper instead of metal. The new method, created by the photographer Fox Talbot, produced a negative image on paper, from which multiple positives could be printed on sensitized paper. Until this breakthrough, multiple copies of a photograph were impossible. The existing daguerreotype process formed an image directly onto a metal plate, with no negative to make additional prints.

According to Alice Augustus persuaded Talbot to teach him the new paper method and learned it with a fellow student referred to as "Lord Russell." When Russell expressed regret that the method had not proven a success in Egypt, Augustus offered to experiment in similar climates in the western hemisphere and, if successful, to send modified formulas to Lord Russell.

The experiments, made on the Island of St. Thomas in the Virgin Islands, where Augustus was guest of the governor, were successful and he sent the promised formulas to England. Sometime later Augustus received an album of photographs from Egypt, proof that the adjustments had worked and that the climatic impediments had been overcome.

Augustus continued his travels sailing to Veracruz, then progressing on horseback across Mexico to Acapulco. He then may have signed aboard a ship to the orient, working as a navigator. Alice noted that he visited Australia, China, and the Pacific islands. By the end of 1851 he had returned to California to make more land transactions. He was in San

Notice of Le Plongeon's photographic business in San Francisco Business Directory for the Year Commencing January 1, 1856, Baggett, Joseph and Company, Publications. Courtesy of the California Historical Society.

Francisco for the 1852 census, in which he was listed as Louis Plongien, occupation—gentleman, born in France.

By 1855 Le Plongeon had established a thriving photographic business in San Francisco. His expertise with the new paper process was becoming a commercial success, according to a notice in the local newspaper announcing the hiring of additional assistants. The studio's success was no surprise to Le Plongeon himself, whose talent for jumping into new territory and finding creative solutions fit right into the scheme of things in gold rush San Francisco.

In 1856 Augustus was elected to the three-year-old

California Academy of Sciences as a resident member. This was indicative of Augustus's experimentation with various professions. He dabbled in law with some success; however, his humanitarian leanings drew him even more strongly to the practice of medicine.

The signature of Augustus Le Plongeon. The three dots found at the end of his name in all his signatures refer to his Masonic membership and is the same as that found at the bottom of his Masonic apron. This signature is from a letter dated 1884, addressed to Stephen Salisbury, Jr. of the American Antiquarian Society.

Augustus may have acquired medical expertise by apprenticing himself to a physician, as was standard practice at the time in the United States. Such an apprenticeship was customarily done in two parts. The first was a reading of basic texts on medicine under the guidance of a doctor. The second was "riding with the doctor," during which time the apprentice gained practical experience. After two or three years of the apprenticeship, the tutor would give his student a certificate of completion and bestow the title *Doctor*. In the mid 1860s Augustus Le Plongeon began using the title on all correspondence and publications. He soon gained renown for successfully treating a variety of difficult cases. And even his foes and rivals addressed him as Dr. Le Plongeon throughout the remainder of his life.

Chapter 2

Perfecting the Image

Ever since the Europeans have known America the attention of the fortune-hunter and the antiquary has been attracted particularly on Peru. It was the treasure-house of the Spaniards in the days of their undisputed control, while for the scholar it has been, and is, a rich field of research.—Alice Le Plongeon in "Early Architecture and Engineering in Peru" (The Engineering Magazine, 1894:46)

The short stay in Chile as a young man had heightened Augustus's appetite for a chance to spend more time in South America. By the early 1860s he had enough money from California land purchases to head south again. This time he went to Peru, perhaps drawn by stories of ruined ancient cities heard during his travels. To support himself he set up a photographic studio.

A short article published in Lima's *El Comercio* on March 27, 1862 announced the opening of the photographic studio of Los Señores Augusto Le Plongeon y Ca., Galería Fotográfica Norte Americana, modeled after American studios. The studio had a special translucent glass light source for proper portrait lighting, as well as equipment from the United States, England, and Germany. The studio offered a special changing room for the ladies and promised prompt service. Augustus listed eleven years of photographic experience and offered the choice of paper photography, daguerreotypes, or ambrotypes.

In addition to running the portrait studio, Augustus spent much of his time in 1862 and 1863 exploring and photographing a number of archaeological sites in Peru. He experimented with the new glass-plate negative process, trying to perfect the techniques he had developed in St. Thomas. Eventually he felt confident of his ability to create good photographic images on-site without a permanent darkroom.

The process was difficult enough under controlled studio conditions. In a remote archaeological site it required creativity, patience, and much trial and error. First Le Plongeon would coat the glass plate with a wet collodion syrup made by dissolving cellulose nitrate, or gun cotton, in a solution of alcohol and ether. He experimented with several formulas of iodide and bromide to be added to the collodion. Then he would sensitize the plate by immersing it in a bath of silver nitrate. After the plate was withdrawn from the bath, it had to be mounted in the camera and exposed, then returned to the darkroom to be developed as quickly as possible. Once prepared, the plate would steadily lose its sensitivity as the ether and alcohol slowly evaporated.

In July 1863 Augustus agreed to assist Ephraim G. Squier, known for his earlier reports on archaeology in the Mississippi Valley, in exploring and photographing the Peruvian ruins. He introduced Squier to a number of his friends who owned land on which ruins were located, accompanied him on several expeditions, and assisted him in various other ways.

When Squier left for New York Le Plongeon entrusted him with a set of glass negatives to hand carry to the publisher Anthony and Company. The material never reached the publisher. Squier apparently kept the negatives to use in his own publications without crediting his collaborator. Le Plongeon would not learn about this upsetting situation for almost a decade. By then it would be too late to do anything.

After he had been in Peru for a time Augustus, a Freemason, felt compelled to speak out against what he thought were abuses by Jesuit priests and the Catholic Church, and wrote two books about religion and the Jesuits in Peru. The first book *La Religión de Jesus Comparada con las Enseñanzas de la Iglesia* was published in 1867. The second *Los Jesuitas e el Peru* appeared in 1869.

At about the same time Augustus established a private medical clinic in Lima where, like many other physicians

Augustus Le Plongeon wearing the Masonic collar used in American Freemasonry and the apron of the Blue Lodge. The original stereo photo may have been a self portrait taken around 1873. No negative has been located and the original print, in poor condition, was restored by Ralph E. Black.

and experimenters, he used the application of electricity in medicinal baths to promote healing of broken bones. Augustus referred to it as "my electro-hydropathic establishment" (1878a).

This interest in electromagnetism led Augustus to a study of earthquakes. He followed one of the accepted scientific thoughts of the day which was based on electromagnetic theory, rather than on an understanding of plate tectonics. He found Peru to be the perfect natural laboratory for studying the causes and effects of earthquakes. Augustus theorized that electromagnetic currents, in conjunction with chemical reactions, caused certain areas under the earth's crust to heat up. Those locations, in turn, would superheat water until it became steam. The resulting tremendous increase in pressure would move the steam through underground channels at high speed, thus disrupting the surface.

Magnetism, wrote Le Plongeon, "is, therefore, the life-sustainer, the soul, of the whole creation, of which our reduced planet is but one of the smallest atoms" (1872:541). These concepts would also apply to living things, he reasoned, and thus could be used for healing purposes. He attempted to do just that in applying galvanic currents to earthquake victims whose injuries he understood to be caused by the destructive effect of electromagnetic energy.

A major source of Le Plongeon's data was the devastating earthquake that hit Peru on August 13, 1868. He observed the event and its aftermath and carefully recorded what he saw. Noting the time of the tremor as exactly 4:46 P.M., he described the oscillatory motion of the repeated shocks and the tidal waves that followed. "The shocks came from the south; the skies were stormy, a very light wind blew from a southerly direction. The whole soil of the country, as far as it could be seen, was moving; first like a wave, from north to south, then it trembled, and at last upheaved heavily" (1872:582). He traveled about the devastated country interviewing victims and recording in detail the damage to many cities. Some were totally destroyed by tidal waves; others were flattened by seismic waves. His writings included observations of apparent animal premonitions occurring before a quake, a summary of seismic activity in Peru since the conquest, and information on the effects of the August 13 tidal wave throughout the Pacific.

During his eight years in Peru Augustus explored many sites on his own, including Tiahuanaco and other prehispanic sites. There was little known at the time about these monumental stone cities, some a thousand years old. Augustus's inclination to jump into the unknown and find an explanation or a solution led him to study and scrutinize the ancient ruins, looking for clues about their builders. He began forming ideas on the origin of world civilization. Until that time few theorists looked to the New World for origins, and most considered it to be, if anything, inferior to the Old World. Contrary to the more commonly held theories, Le Plongeon came to believe that the cradle of world civilization was in the New World.

He was familiar with the writings of the French scholar Brasseur de Bourbourg, whose history of New World civilizations hypothesized that all civilization originated in the Americas. There was also Stephens and Catherwood's descriptions of the magnificent ruins in Yucatan and Central America. As Le Plongeon's knowledge developed, it became apparent to him that ancient civilizations in Mexico should be investigated. Perhaps the ancient Maya cities held the answers to his questions.

Augustus felt compelled to share the information he had amassed in Peru with the scholars he knew back in California. They would surely be as excited as he was about such natural phenomena and exotic civilizations. In 1870

Le Plongeon returned by boat to San Francisco, where he made several appearances before the California Academy of Sciences. On August 15 he lectured on some "remarkable" Peruvian skulls. On September 5 he read part of a long article on the aboriginal ruins of Peru and exhibited artifacts and architectural photographs showing the use of the arch.

On December 5 and 19 he read a long essay about his theories on seismology. This work also appeared in an article, "The Causes of Earthquakes," published in 1872 in Van Nostrand's *Eclectric Engineering Magazine.* In it Augustus wrote that the earthquake that devastated Peru in 1868 was a result of the action of percolated sea water and "chemical elements" that had reached a critical heat level. They were made "incandescent" because that location of chemical activity coincided with "the voltaic arch formed by the electro-magnetic current passing between the sun as positive element and the earth as negative."

After his appearances before the California Academy of Sciences Le Plongeon traveled to New York to lecture on his work in Peru and to try to sell several paintings he had acquired there. In March 1871 he exhibited these works, two by Bartolomé Esteban Murillo and one by his teacher, the master Juan del Castillo. The *New York Evening Mail* covered the event in a front-page article titled "Three Important Paintings from Peru."

Shortly after that Augustus left for London to study an old Spanish manuscript in the British Museum which he hoped would help unlock some secret of ancient New World civilization. It was to be an eventful trip, since a visit to London and Paris always had to include some social obligations and diversions. Sometime in the course of the year Augustus met Alice Dixon of Regents Park in London. Though not yet twenty the well-bred young woman displayed remarkable poise and self-confidence. Her questioning spirit must have caught Augustus's fancy, for the seasoned explorer, twenty-five years her senior, began courting her. Her parents, Henry and Sophia Dixon, were impressed with him as a tough man of the world, yet of a gentlemanly French background. His descriptions of far-flung places and mysterious lost civilizations captured Alice's imagination and intellect, and his kind-hearted, understanding manner captured her heart.

Alice Dixon and Augustus Le Plongeon were married before leaving for New York in January 1873. Alice bid farewell to her parents and four brothers and sisters, promising her dear sister Lucy that she would write often.

No sooner had Augustus returned to New York with

11

Alice Dixon Le Plongeon, circa 1875, photographed in the romantic style of the day, probably in Merida. 5 × 8 inch.

his young bride than he became embroiled in controversy. He contacted Harper's Brothers about publishing an article based on his research in Peru, intending to use the photographs E. G. Squier was to have carried to New York for him in 1863. The publisher told him to consult with Squier, since they already had a contract with him, which included publication of the photographs Squier was now claiming as his own.

Augustus was crushed by this apparent breach of confidence by someone he had collaborated with so closely. He agonized over how to handle the situation. Any hope of righting the matter slipped away within a few months, when Squier was declared mentally incompetent. Augustus had no evidence to substantiate his claim that the photographs were actually his. Even though he had used some of them in previous lectures at the California Academy of Sciences they were not published or recorded anywhere in his name.

And they were undeniably in Squier's possession.

Squier must have had good connections, because it seemed not to matter that he had previously been involved in a similar controversy over stealing authorship from a colleague. An 1847 report to the Smithsonian Institution about research done by Squier and Edwin H. Davis listed Squier as author and Davis as his assistant on a forthcoming book, *Ancient Monuments of the Mississippi Valley*. Before the book came out, it took tremendous professional pressure from the Smithsonian authorities to persuade Squier to share the authorship with Davis. Squier insisted that "only his generosity and friendship continued the partnership in which he alone produced anything" (Tax 1973:201).

Squier's intransigence, however annoying, did not ruin all of Le Plongeon's plans in New York. He appeared before the New York Geographical Society to read a scientific paper and he published a comprehensive manual of photography in Spanish that he had begun in Peru. The two-hundred-page book *Manual de Fotografía* covered all the materials and formulas used by a professional photographer of the 1870s. By then the daguerreotype process Augustus had used in California was being supplanted by the wet collodion glass-plate negative process, which had become his standard practice in the field. Le Plongeon described in great detail the darkroom, cameras and their operation, preparation and action of chemicals, and the method of development, fixing, washing, and drying of negatives. With as much precision as possible he described the art of preparing collodion glass-plate negatives.

The *Manual* included a trouble-shooting section and guidelines to help the photographer. His final admonition, spoken from experience, was that the photographer needed to become totally familiar with his own camera equipment, chemicals, and the varied environment in order to make a perfect image.

With the photographic manual completed and professional and social contacts made in New York, the Le Plongeons were making plans to explore the archaeological ruins of Mexico. They were anxious to delve into the secrets of the ancient Maya.

Chapter 3

Stepping into a
Hostile World

The fact is that ever since the 16th century, when the conquest was said to be effected, the people have from time to time renewed their vain struggle, till, in 1847, after a long contest and many scenes of horror, a few thousand freed themselves from all government save the authority of their chiefs. From that time to this they have waged war against all the other inhabitants, and though many expeditions have been organized against them, they have not for one moment been reduced to obedience.—Alice Le Plongeon in "Conquest of the Mayas" (Magazine of American History 19:120)

Augustus was soon putting his ingenuity and photographic techniques to a field test more rigorous than ever before. In July 1873 he and Alice sailed for the Yucatan peninsula of Mexico where they would contend with heat, humidity, insects, scarce water supplies, makeshift darkrooms set up inside remote Maya ruins, and the threat of attack by hostile local factions of rebellious Maya.

After a few days at sea and a stop in Cuba, their vessel anchored off the Yucatan port of Progreso—the signs were ominous.

ꓓ ꓓ ꓓ

In 1873 Yucatan was a land divided by rebellion. The northwestern corner of the peninsula, including Merida the capital, was under the control of Mexican federal troops. It was the only portion in which it was considered safe to travel. Most of the remaining territory, including Campeche and Quintana Roo, was controlled by Maya rebels who had retreated there two decades earlier after nearly taking Merida. They came to be known as the Chan Santa Cruz Maya, or Cruzob, taking their name from a symbol of their rebellion, a small cross said to be invested with special powers. This armed struggle by the Maya to drive the foreigners from their homeland came to be known as the War of the Castes. It had seemed almost inevitable from the earliest days of the conquest in the sixteenth century.

The excesses of the Spanish church, the cruel tactics of the military, and the harsh exploitations possible under the hacienda system were elements in the suppression of the Maya spirit during the centuries following the conquest. Spanish priests tore down Maya temples and burned their sacred books, saying they were pictures of the devil. The hacienda system imposed by the conquerors robbed the Maya of their sacred land, then placed them in slave labor to the new Spanish land owners. The military meted out its own form of swift and final punishment.

As the decades wore on and the Maya passed down stories of their heritage—the glorious cities of Uxmal, Chichen Itza, Coba—a particularly heinous event stood out. The Maya kept alive the memory of an attempted rebellion in 1761, when Jacinto Canek led his men in a vain effort to drive the foreigners from their homeland. Canek paid a severe price; he was drawn and quartered, his parts burned, and the ashes scattered. Eight of his most important lieutenants were garrotted, and two hundred were whipped and had one ear cut off to identify them forever as rebels.

In 1847 when rebellion again broke out, Jacinto Canek's name was the rallying cry. This time the Maya rebels were well organized and determined to drive the Spanish, and mestizos (their mixed-blood descendants) into the sea. For two years they pushed toward Merida, taking town after town, finally laying siege on the capital itself.

Then, just as complete victory was in their hands and the residents of Merida were preparing to evacuate by boats from Progreso, the Maya stopped. Winged ants had appeared in great numbers, signaling the coming of the rains. Despite the pleas of their leaders, the Maya soldiers withdrew to their villages and fields. Had the rebels stayed one more month, Yucatan would have reverted to the Maya. But the government used that time to reinforce and recover ground. Troops from Mexico were brought to Yucatan in great numbers and the Maya were pushed back to a line running approximately north-south between Chichen Itza and Valladolid. Yucatan was effectively cut in half. Travel was relatively safe in areas near Merida, Uxmal to the south, and Izamal to the east; but once the traveler got twenty-five or so miles beyond, an ambush or even a siege of a town was very possible.

⌐⌐ ⌐⌐ ⌐⌐

On August 6, 1873, two days after leaving the island of Cuba, Alice and Augustus Le Plongeon had their first glimpse of the low, level plain of the Yucatan coast. Alice was struck by the flat monotony of the landscape bathed in the bright morning sunlight. The lush vegetation looked inviting, but the long-planned arrival faced unforeseen obstacles. "The first sound from the land that reached our ear was the sharp, shrill call of the bugle—ill omen for the peace of the country," Alice wrote in the diary that was to be her constant companion for many years in the field.

A customshouse boat drew alongside their steamer, the *Cuba,* and a health officer and the American Consul Martin Hatch came on board. Mr. Hatch told them that yellow fever, carried by rainy-season mosquitoes, was wreaking havoc among the foreigners in Merida. Indeed, he had just lost his father to it. The health officer warned them that it was unusually severe that season among the people not acclimated. The Consul advised them not to land.

Equally distressing to them was the news that Yucatan was in a state of revolution with frequent encounters between federal troops and Maya rebels. But the Le Plongeons were not about to turn back. Augustus had been priming Alice for this great step for two years. "Not withstanding this rather discouraging news, having started to see Yucatan, we left the steamer about 8 o'clock, A.M. on board a lighter," Alice wrote. "As the weather was very calm, it took us three hours, under scorching sun, to reach the land." After their landing at Progreso the Le Plongeons traveled to Merida, a few hours away by a rough carriage road cut through fields of henequen [a spiny agave whose fibers were used for making rope]. They passed well-tended haciendas growing sugarcane and henequen in territory firmly controlled by government troops.

Once in Merida the Le Plongeons settled into the Hotel Meridiano, the only hotel at the time, according to Alice, and began to explore the bustling capital of Yucatan. They were favorably impressed by the layout of the city, especially the plazas with their flower beds, iron benches, and marble walkways. The uninitiated visitor could not have guessed that Merida had almost become a battleground two decades

17

earlier or that those conditions still existed all too closely in the countryside of Yucatan.

A major social event in Merida was the weekly orchestra concert set in the old tree-lined Plaza de Jesús. A few days after their arrival the Le Plongeons attended one of these concerts. Alice was favorably impressed by the band, the balmy evening, and the graceful ladies. "Dressed, nearly all of them, in white, they glided, rather than walked, to the compas [rhythm] of harmonious sounds. We have never seen any people move as gracefully as do the Yucatecan ladies."

Their enjoyment of Merida was short lived; one week after the Le Plongeons arrived, the dreaded yellow fever struck Alice. For a week she lay seriously ill in the hotel, attended by her husband, "who patiently fulfilled the duties of nurse and physician with the most assiduous care, not sleeping, during seven days, more than an hour in every twenty-four, as we had been assured that no stranger attacked with the fever that year had escaped death." But under Augustus's loving care, Alice beat the odds and survived the fever.

When Alice had recovered sufficiently they moved to more permanent accommodations in Merida and began long months of research in the vicinity. Alice needed time to recover fully and they both had to get acclimated. They studied nearby ruins of pyramids, getting a clearer picture of the relationship of the various sites, determining their condition, and noting features such as hieroglyphic inscriptions and carved figures that might lead to further research.

Since they were not in Yucatan merely to photograph and survey the archaeological sites as a number of travelers had done earlier, they spent a great deal of time searching the archives in Merida. They were there to unravel the meaning of a civilization long since abandoned. This required extensive knowledge of the history, ethnology, linguistics, ecology, and archaeology of the area. Augustus wanted to test his theory of New World origins. He professed a desire to judge for himself rather than follow theories advanced by others.

Augustus and Alice learned to speak Yucatec Maya and became acquainted with local scholars and many Maya speakers. One of their tutors was Father Crescencio Carillo y Ancona, a Maya priest who was later to become Bishop of Yucatan. They saw their ability to communicate with the living Maya as an important step to interpreting the past. In this way they hoped the messages written in hieroglyphics at the sites they were visiting would become intelligible to

them. "I prefer to listen to the mute yet eloquent voices of the painters, sculptors, and architects, who have written the history of their nation on the stones of the monuments reared to perpetuate and make known to succeeding generations the events recorded by them," said Augustus Le Plongeon (1879:69).

During the 1873–74 dry season the Le Plongeons paid their first of several visits to the ancient abandoned city of Uxmal. Nestled at the northern edge of the Puuc hills, about forty miles south of Merida, it was the most accessible and most visited of the larger Maya ruins in Yucatan. It was also safely inside government-controlled territory, beyond the reach of raids by Maya rebels.

Alice and Augustus set out from Merida very early one morning, passing dozens of men and women on their way to market. Some were on horseback, some carried embroidered blouses on their heads, and some pulled carts full of ramon branches [a type of nut tree] for fodder. The Le Plongeons and their photographic equipment rode in a *volan coche,* a large wheeled wagon "very suitable for the roads of Yucatan, that, with few exceptions, are like a stormy sea petrified. Three mules and a driver make this conveyance go good speed" (Alice Le Plongeon 1885:374).

Despite the heat and humidity Alice dressed in a high-necked, full-length Victorian dress, the mode of the day.

Alice's working dress: a skirt over cotton pants, which she could roll up while working in the ruins. Around the local women she could roll the skirt down. This photo, taken among the stones of a tumbled-down vault in the Akab Dzib at Chichen Itza, shows her at about age twenty-two. She still wore her hair in ringlets. Augustus Le Plongeon's 1875 stereo photo has been enlarged and cropped by L. G. Desmond.

19

Later she adopted pants covered by a skirt. The conservative Maya women would have been scandalized by a woman in pants, so she wore the skirt over them when in the presence of the Maya and rolled it up around her waist when working in the ruins.

The first stop outside Merida was Abala, about twenty-four miles to the south, where they took some photographs and spent the night. The next day they reached the village of Muna, fifteen miles north of Uxmal. There at the community well, they watched the women drawing water from a trough filled continuously by a simple mechanical device powered by a mule. The women gave a handful of maize to the animal for each jug of water drawn.

The Le Plongeons stayed for a time in Muna, photographing the sixteenth-century church and the village of adobe buildings and thatch-roofed Maya huts, using 5 × 8 inch glass plates. They also explored the caves that honey-combed the limestone hills nearby. When their work was completed they left for Uxmal by the old route skirting the Puuc hills which were the only visible break in the even sea of green flowing to Progreso on the north coast.

In the 1870s the archaeological site of Uxmal was part of a sugarcane and cattle-producing hacienda. Its principal residence stood within a large enclosure, where cattle drank from stone troughs. The hacienda employed about five hundred workers, whose minuscule salaries often led to a sort of enslavement to the hacienda store. Because of this extreme poverty, "they live and die in abject misery," Alice lamented. She was moved by their plight and vowed to make the world aware of the Maya's situation by writing about them for the American press. She would continue this effort throughout her life, writing for such publications as The *New York World, Popular Science,* and The *Magazine of American History.*

During their first short visit to Uxmal, Alice and Augustus were struck by the magnitude of the ruined Maya city. They camped in the Governor's Palace, sleeping in hammocks slung over beams spanning the corbelled arches inside.

They noted that in 1842 Stephens and Catherwood had ordered the brush cleared from the monuments so they could make a general plan of the ruins. The plan was correct as far as it went, the Le Plongeons discovered, but the remains extended much farther in every direction. To undertake a similar brush clearing was considered "a thing today impracticable, except at a large expense" (Alice Le Plongeon 1881b:2). To photograph and survey only the most important structures at Uxmal was an enormous undertaking,

requiring a number of weeks. The clearing would have to be repeated on each subsequent visit. They took some 5 × 8 inch photos and made plans to return for a more detailed photographic survey.

⊓ ⊓ ⊓

The Le Plongeons' work and travels became well known in Merida. A year after their arrival an outbreak of smallpox was racing through the peninsula. Dr. Le Plongeon was approached in a panic by the governor of Yucatan, Dr. Liborio Irigoyen, who begged him to vaccinate for smallpox whenever he saw the need, since the epidemic was out of control. The treasury was too depleted by the War of the Castes to pay the doctor any salary, but Le Plongeon readily agreed. Under this mandate Alice and Augustus scrutinized the area, traveling for a year to a myriad of lesser sites and towns in the vicinity of Uxmal.

This task gave them a welcome excuse to attend a number of religious and secular festivals and observe the customs of the people. Alice wrote detailed accounts of their local practices. They also saw that the Indians regarded the ceremonies of their forefathers with far more veneration than

Maya women grinding corn with mano and metate, circa 1875. The Le Plongeons spent time in Maya villages to learn the language and customs of the people whose ancestors they were studying. Alice felt compelled to publish reports of their living conditions, especially on the haciendas. Stereo.

21

The Le Plongeons attended a fiesta at Izamal. They photographed dancers and musicians in the arcaded plaza. Circa 1875. Stereo.

those forced upon them for three centuries by the Catholic priests. One of these was the *Etzmeek Nylan,* performed as a rite of passage when a child reached four months of age. A woman chosen for the occasion became a sort of godmother, and her symbolic act was to carry the child on her hip. Alice observed the ceremony and how it was believed to shape the child's future.

> After the child is placed astride the hip, the woman walks round the outside of the house five times with the baby. Five eggs are buried in hot ashes, that they may there break, and the child thus have its five senses awakened. If the eggs do not break readily, it is a sure sign that the children will not be very intelligent. If they wish to write well, they place a pen in its hand during the ceremony; to read well, a book; to work in the fields, a machete (1879:94).

Other ceremonies, such as curing rites based on the traditional use of medicinal herbs, could also be observed in the towns and villages of Yucatan. But not everything followed Maya tradition, Alice noted. "The ancient H-Men (wise man) was possibly a sage of great learning, but the H-Men of today is a trickster and imposter."

22

The more Augustus and Alice observed the Maya people, the more they realized that the current residents of Yucatan were the direct descendants of the ancient Maya who had built the once magnificent temples and pyramids. Could those ancient American people be the source of civilization to the whole world? Augustus had already seen some evidence at Uxmal, and heard about the ancient city of Chichen Itza which had been visited by Stephens and Catherwood, and the photographer Désiré Charnay a number of years before. It had many bas-relief carvings; perhaps they would hold a clue.

Chapter 4

A Turning Point

I had really scarcely commenced my studies, notwithstanding I had worked every day from sunrise to sunset, so many and important were the monuments that, very superficially, my predecessors had visited.—Augustus Le Plongeon in "Doctor Le Plongeon in Yucatan" (Salisbury 1877:84)

If Augustus Le Plongeon was to prove his theory of the origin of civilization in the New World, he had to study the Maya city of Chichen Itza, abandoned hundreds of years earlier. It was equally as large and as important to him as Uxmal. But there was a major problem getting to the site. In 1875 the territory around Chichen Itza was controlled by the Chan Santa Cruz Maya, who were still waging guerilla warfare against the government.

It was a standoff between two cultures and two worlds. On the one hand were the traditional Maya who saw their ties to the land being broken by forced migrations into towns and haciendas. Their leaders had retreated to remote areas of Quintana Roo where they rallied support around a cult that waited for prophecies from an oracle who spoke through a sacred Speaking Cross. On the other hand were those of Spanish background who controlled the government and the Maya who had accepted their presence.

25

In the spring of that year, despite warnings from government officials, the Le Plongeons made their way toward Chichen Itza. They circled north of it, arriving on May 20 at the government-held town of Valladolid a few miles to the east. Within the old colonial town they were relatively safe.

All summer their efforts to reach Chichen Itza, only a few miles away, were stymied by the lack of a military escort and the constant reports of guerrillas in the area. While they waited, the Le Plongeons gathered information about the Maya and their beliefs. In the town of Espita the curate, Padre Domínguez, introduced them to a very old man named Mariano Chablé, said by some to have reached the astounding age of one hundred fifty years. Augustus, who had not yet perfected his Maya, interviewed the man with the aid of a Spanish-Maya interpreter.

The conversation left Augustus with two important pieces of information that helped shape his research at Chichen Itza. The first was that a man named Manuel Alayón, who died in 1835, "had a book that none could read," a "sacred book." They must be referring to a codex, Augustus thought. This gave him the hope that he might find one of the sacred Maya picture books still intact. The second was a statement by Chablé about a hieroglyphic text in the Akab Dzib, a many-chambered building at Chichen Itza. Le Plongeon related this and other events and findings in field reports to Stephen Salisbury, Jr. of the American Antiquarian Society, who published them in the *Proceedings* of the society.

Le Plongeon understood Chablé to say that the text spoke of a day in the future "when inhabitants of Saci (Valladolid) would converse with those of Ho (Merida) by means of a cord, that would be stretched by people not belonging to the country" (Salisbury 1877:117). Le Plongeon reasoned that since old Chablé had no knowledge of the telegraph, there must be something to the story, since the informant had no reason to deceive him. Instead Chablé may have been telling Augustus the Maya legend of a cosmic umbilical cord that was thought to connect Maya cities to the gods. Augustus made a mental note to search for the Akab Dzib as soon as he arrived at Chichen Itza.

On September 21 General Palomino, later to become governor of Yucatan, finally completed arrangements for a military escort to Chichen Itza. Accompanying the Le Plongeons on their journey from Valladolid to Chichen Itza were Colonel Felipe Díaz, commander of the eastern defense line—known as the "Line of the East," Colonel José Coronado, and two companies of soldiers.

The entourage arrived at Dzitas, ten miles north of Chichen Itza, only to find the path to Piste, a deserted village with a military post near the site, completely overgrown. Colonel Coronado set his men to the task of clearing the route and a few days later, after a six-hour journey on foot from Dzitas, the Le Plongeons and their party arrived in Piste without incident.

There, nestled around a cenote, they saw the remains of what had been a pretty village ten years earlier. On election Sunday 1865 the peaceful beauty of the village with its thatch-roofed houses, citrus trees, and kitchen gardens had been shaken by an attack of the Chan Santa Cruz Maya. They came to avenge anyone they thought had cooperated with their enemy, the government. The village was destroyed that day, and only a few of its residents, taking refuge in the bush, escaped the terrible machete blows.

Now the roofless houses, their walls crumbling, lay nearly hidden, overcome by the thick forest. Augustus was moved by the sight of the church which had been converted into a fortress for the handful of soldiers stationed there.

> The church alone sad and melancholy, without
> doors, its sanctuaries silent, its floor paved with the
> burial slabs of the victims, surrounded by parapets,
> yet stands in the midst of the ruined adobes of
> those who used to gather under its roof. Its old
> walls, its belfry, widowed of its bells, are all that
> indicates to the traveler that Piste once was there.
> (Salisbury 1877:83–84).

After resting and exchanging news with the soldiers at Piste, the Le Plongeons and their escort continued their march to Chichen Itza. Long before they reached the site, they could see the tallest pyramid, El Castillo, towering over the green canopy "as a solitary light-house in the midst of the ocean." Night had already fallen when they reached the principal house of the Hacienda Chichen, which Colonel Coronado had ordered cleaned for their use. Alice and Augustus could hardly sleep that night, anticipating the days of discovery and hard work that lay ahead.

The next day Colonel Díaz had the house fortified and lookouts placed strategically atop some of the higher structures to provide a warning if attack came from the Chan Santa Cruz who continued to scout the area.

Colonel Díaz soon reported that the Chan Santa Cruz were about to attack and urged withdrawal from Chichen Itza. Le Plongeon refused. "I made known my unalterable resolution to Colonel Díaz, asking him only to arm a few

*The Akab Dzib, Chichen Itza,
1875. Workers have cleared
the vegetation so the Le Plongeons could photograph and
map the structure. The lintel
with the hieroglyphic text is
inside the door to the right of
the workmen. Stereo.*

of the Indians that remained with me, for I did not wish even a single soldier of the post of Piste to accompany me." Perhaps, too, Alice and Augustus felt they were protected by some mystical force, or perhaps their deepening empathy for the Maya gave them a sense of security.

They made the church at Piste their headquarters, walking to the site each morning. At night they returned to Piste, leaving their photographic and measuring equipment at the ruins a league away. Augustus had already realized that his estimate of three weeks to investigate the ruins, based on previous travelers' reports, was insufficient. He and Alice wanted to complete a more detailed study of the monumental limestone structures than had their predecessors.

Augustus was anxious to track down the Akab Dzib, "the house of dark writing," so he could examine the hieroglyphic text Chablé had described. He found the building deep in the brush behind the spiral-shaped observatory, known as the Caracol. The Akab Dzib was a small west-facing building with two wings housing a series of rooms. The east side, a stone-faced foundation as high as the building, had been added by its builders, apparently for a second story that was never finished.

The stone lintel Augustus was seeking lay atop the door to an interior room in the west wing. It was carved with glyphs on the front and the portrait of a Maya ruler underneath. As soon as Augustus located and cleared the lintel, he excitedly began his interpretation of it. To his astonishment he saw glyphs that, to him, represented lightning or electricity. His interpretation of the glyphs included a reference to the cord Chablé had told him about in Espita. This important find had to be thoroughly recorded and

documented, so Augustus set up his photographic equipment for the difficult task. No direct sunlight reached the doorway, although the afternoon sun cast some light into the room.

After much trial and error he succeeded in producing a good negative using a long exposure. "With care I washed the slab, then with black crayon darkened its surface until the intaglio letters appeared in white on a dark background." He took the photo in stereo to further enhance its clarity and made a mold of the Maya writing that supposedly foretold the invention of the telegraph.[1]

Augustus wrote of his interpretation both to the president of Mexico, Sebastian Lerdo de Tejada, and to Stephen Salisbury, Jr. He noted that the text was "said to be a prophecy." His interpretation was published in the *Proceedings of the American Antiquarian Society* in 1877, and soon thereafter those who were eager to find fault with his work claimed that Dr. Le Plongeon believed the Maya *used* the telegraph for communication.

Augustus drew a detailed and accurate floor plan of the Akab Dzib, noting tunneling in four of the rooms.[2] In the drawing he hypothesized a mirror image of the west central structure, represented by dashed lines in the center of the core area. He must have observed the filled-in rooms on the second level of the nearby Monjas, or Nunnery, structure and conjectured that a similar method was used to provide a foundation for a second level on the Akab Dzib. He noted that the northeast corner of the structure had collapsed since Frederick Catherwood drew it in 1842.

In order to photograph the various buildings, Le Plongeon had to deal with the same monumental problem faced

Le Plongeon's 1875 stereo photo of the hieroglyphic text in the Akab Dzib at Chichen Itza was made in extremely low light. He highlighted the relief carvings, then made a long exposure as afternoon light filtered in to the interior lintel. He used the photo to inform the American Antiquarian Society that a drawing made by Frederick Catherwood was "mere lines (many of them imaginary)," and that attempts to interpret it resulted in pure "nonsense" (Augustus Le Plongeon 1881b:250).

Opposite page:

Top: A rare shot of Alice and Augustus together, taken on the southeast corner of the second level of Las Monjas, Chichen Itza, circa 1875. A soldier stands in the doorway behind them. Photography was by remote shutter release or by an assistant. Stereo.

Middle: Alice poses with her rifle before the east facade of Las Monjas Annex. Her Maya workers point to the Itzamna figure above the door inside of what Augustus called the "cosmic egg." The non-Maya men in the photo are not identified, but the man to the right of the doorway with hand gun and machete is probably an officer from their military escort. Stereo.

Bottom: La Iglesia, Chichen Itza, 1875. Alice sits to the left of the building, behind the workers, who have cleared the trees. The upper right corner of the facade is now missing. Stereo.

by his predecessors: clearing the jungle. He hired local Maya men with machetes to cut down the heavy growth that extended to the tops of the buildings.

As his loyal Maya soldiers stood guard, Augustus began photographing the most important structures. With Alice's expert assistance he made five hundred stereoscopic photos, including close-ups of what he thought were important iconographic details. They concentrated much of their effort on the east wing of the Monjas, photographing its extraordinary facade from several angles to highlight the elaborately carved details. They also photographed La Iglesia with its ornate roof comb.

⌐」 ⌐」 ⌐」

The Le Plongeons' work at Chichen Itza included tracing a number of murals and making molds of bas-reliefs in the Upper and Lower Temple of the Jaguars at the edge of the Ball Court, or Gymnasium, as it was called at the time. Augustus considered this the most interesting building in Chichen Itza, from a historical perspective, and pronounced the bas-reliefs as "having nothing to envy in the bas-reliefs of Assyria and Babylon" (Salisbury 1877:85). He made a composite stereo photo of the bas-reliefs in the Lower Temple of the Jaguars, using his large format, two-lensed camera. He was happy with the crisp detail of the prints and knew that stereo viewing would provide additional detail.[3]

In October and November of 1875 Alice and Augustus concentrated on the Upper Temple. Augustus instructed the workers to remove rubble from the collapsed roof that had nearly filled the outer room and blocked access to the murals in the interior room. Under the rubble was a large stone slab supported by pedestals carved to represent atlantean figures with upturned arms. Augustus photographed and made molds of the reliefs on the columns in the entrance, the carved lintel, the Atlantes, and the altar table which had been broken by the falling roof.

Alice and Augustus studied and began to copy what remained of the murals within the Upper Temple room. They showed vivid scenes of village life, religious events, warfare, and rulers. After studying the scenes in the murals, Augustus concluded that they showed the history of a single generation of Maya rulers at Chichen Itza.[4] He took animal representations to be their totems or spirits. An eagle, which he identified as a macaw, became the symbol for a Maya princess, one of the central characters. She became Queen Móo, after the Maya word for *macaw*. Her brother was named *powerful warrior*, or Prince Chaacmol, a reference to the

When rubble from the collapsed arch of the Upper Temple of the Jaguars was removed, Augustus found these Atlantes and table in the doorway to the inner room. Inside, the walls were covered with murals. In addition to this general view of the artifacts showing the table in situ just behind the great pillars, Le Plongeon photographed each sculpture individually, 1875. Now, the Atlantes have all been removed; some remain at Chichen Itza, some are in the Museum of Anthropology in Merida. 5 × 8 inch.

jaguar whose spots appeared on a shield in the mural and in bas-reliefs on the side of the temple.

Through intrigue and murder, according to his interpretation, Queen Móo was forced to flee to Egypt. On her arrival she was recognized as a long-lost sister, thus proving, as far as Augustus was concerned, that Egyptian civilization had been originated by the ancient Maya.

While the Queen Móo story, which Augustus clung to and expanded over the years, was later to reap him much derision, it did lead him to an important discovery that first season at Chichen Itza. Whether by sheer coincidence or by brilliant deductive reasoning, Augustus used the murals to choose the spot where an important statue lay deeply buried.

> In tracing the figure of Chaacmol in battle, I remarked that the shield worn by him had painted on it round green spots, and was exactly like the ornaments placed between tiger and tiger on the entablature of the same monument. I naturally concluded that the monument had been raised to the memory of the warrior bearing the shield (1881a:16).

This reminded him of a ruined mound he had seen a few days earlier about one hundred yards away in a thicket. "It was ornamented with slabs engraved with the images of spotted tigers, eating human hearts, forming magnificent bas-reliefs, conserving yet traces of the colors in which it was formerly painted."

32

"Prince Coh in Battle." Tracing from the Upper Temple of the Jaguars mural, Chichen Itza, 1883. Tracing and interpretation by Alice and Augustus Le Plongeon. Though their identification of the murals as depictions of Maya history may be correct, the story they created went far beyond the evidence. However, their tracings compare favorably with the later, more well-known work of Adela Breton.

Led by the stones that "speak to those who can understand them" and "inspired perhaps also by the instinct of the archaeologist" (Salisbury 1877:86), Augustus returned with the trusted worker, Desiderio Kansal, to the small mound. As they began to clear the brush, a slab emerged, showing a reclining jaguar with the same round dots Augustus had seen on the murals. "My interpretations had been correct," he explained in a letter to President Tejada. "Everything I saw proved it to me. I at once concentrated all my attention at this spot."

Le Plongeon ordered his workers to begin digging carefully into the mound, later called the Platform of the Eagles and Jaguars. Deep within it they found a large stone sculpture of a reclining figure, which Le Plongeon immediately identified as the Maya prince, Chaacmol, youngest brother and consort of Queen Móo.

The excavation of the statue, some five feet long and

33

The Platform of the Eagles and Jaguars prior to its excavation by the Le Plongeons, 1875. Alice and workers sit on the mound, cleared of vegetation. Stereo.

weighing several hundred pounds, was no easy task. According to Augustus's calculations it lay more than twenty feet deep amid hundreds of loose stones. He was well aware of the danger involved. "I possessed no tools, nor machines of any description. I resorted to the machete of my Indians, the trees of the forest, and the vines that entwine their trunks. I formed a frame-work to prevent the falling of the stones."

With the assistance of his Maya workmen, he constructed an inclined plane and a capstan to hold the rope for pulling the statue from the deep excavation. A tree trunk served as a fulcrum, with a pole as a lever. With Le Plongeon's careful planning, after some sleepless nights wondering if the sculpture could ever be retrieved, it took his ten men only half an hour to raise it to the surface.

Years later archaeologist Edward H. Thompson, the American consul in Merida, related an interview he had with the grandson of Desiderio Kansal. The young Maya recalled that all the men accompanied Augustus to the mound. "I, the young son of my father, stood by his knee listening to the words of my father's father. Listening, I remembered and remembering, later understood." He could still picture "the bearded white one" plucking at his long beard and giving orders where to dig. After the statue appeared, Le Plongeon told them to dig at another spot.

> "As they dug, the figures of Bacabes (minor gods) rose out of the ground as if to meet the bearded white one. He looked at them long and thoughtfully, plucking at his beard, and as he looked at the Bacabes, we saw that his lips were moving. Then we who saw these things said to each

other, 'Doubtless he is speaking to them' "
(Thompson 1931:341–342).

Juan Peón Contreras, director of Merida's Museo Yucateco, recounted his version of how Le Plongeon located the Chaacmol. "By abstruse archaeological reasoning, and by his meditation, [he] determined the place, and, striking the spot with his foot, he said, 'Here it is, here it will be found' " (Salisbury 1877:93).

The excavation also uncovered a number of artifacts associated with the statue. A bowl carved on the chest of the figure contained a broken flint blade, a jade bead, and organic material that Le Plongeon thought was from the cremated heart of Prince Chaacmol. Le Plongeon collected the material and took it to Charles Thompson, professor of chemistry at the Worcester Free Institute. Thompson analyzed the material and declared it "once part of a human body which has been burned with some fuel." At the base of the statue were eighteen flint projectile points including seven of green stone, two flat ceramic plates, and a ceramic pot. Augustus took a jadeite tube, also from the urn, and mounted it in a gold brooch as a gift for Alice. It became her "talisman of Queen Móo," a symbol of Alice's spiritual connection with the queen of Chichen Itza.

Stephen Salisbury, who edited Augustus's reports from the field into an article on "Dr. Le Plongeon in Yucatan," changed the spelling of Chaacmol to Chacmool, a Maya term for puma, not realizing that Le Plongeon had created his own term from two distinct Maya words, *chaac,* and *mol* for *powerful warrior.* Salisbury's spelling of Chacmool became

Augustus Le Plongeon posed, reclining, on the Chaacmol. The discovery of this statue at Chichen Itza may have been the single most crucial event in setting the course of the Le Plongeons' further fieldwork. Photograph by Alice Le Plongeon, 1875. Stereo.

Augustus took several portaits of Alice with Queen Móo's talisman worn prominently as a brooch. Augustus had the piece fashioned from a jadeite tube found in a stone urn uncovered near the head of the Chaacmol statue in the Platform of the Eagles and Jaguars. Alice wore the talisman as a symbol of her spiritual connection with Queen Móo of Chichen Itza. The talisman is now lost.
5 × 8 inch, circa 1885.

the accepted name for Le Plongeon's statue and similar ones which were later uncovered elsewhere. Le Plongeon eventually accepted Salisbury's translation, but in an act of linguistic one-upmanship, used *coh* in later writings, a more common Maya word with the same meaning.

With the discovery of the Chacmool Augustus was convinced that he had correctly interpreted the murals in the Upper Temple of the Jaguars. This success gave him confidence in his ability to reconstruct the history of the Maya which, in turn he hoped, would provide the key to unlock even greater mysteries of the world. This line of reasoning in his research was gaining a momentum that would be difficult to curtail.

Chapter 5

Face-Off and Retreat

When evening came, and all from work reposed,
They told the white man why the things inclosed
Were found by him: "Thou art returned once more
From long enchanted sleep; wast here before."
To this, both earnestly responded—"Nay,"
But nothing changed; the men thought their own way.
—Alice Le Plongeon in "Queen Móo's Talisman" (1902:71)

Augustus and Alice were constantly reminded of the potential danger in the circumstances that surrounded them. They were working in an isolated location, made more remote because the Chan Santa Cruz Maya controlled all but one route of communication. And their Maya guards and workers must have felt some sympathy toward the rebel cause, or at least feared retribution from the gods or the Cruzob for meddling in what was considered to be sacred ground. Some Maya towns had been burned to the ground because residents were thought to be aiding the enemy.

Augustus, however, felt he had the power to control the situation. But he needed to persuade his workers of his special relationship to the site, perhaps as a reincarnated ruler. He knew that he bore a noticeable resemblance to a certain bearded figure portrayed on a door jamb atop El Castillo. They were sure to be impressed if they thought it

was actually his portrait. And it was a way to test his suspicion that they and their ancestors believed in reincarnation as did the Egyptians. One day Augustus led them with great mystery and ceremony to the summit of the great pyramid. In the outside room on the north side he showed them the profile of a warrior wearing a long pointed beard. "I placed my head against the stone so as to present the same position of my face as that of Uxan and called the attention of my Indians to the similarity of his and my own features" (1881a:54). They were instantly persuaded, as illustrated by the story Desiderio Kansal related to his grandson. "We saw that the faces of the two were as the face of one. Then we said one to the other, 'Doubtless they are one'" (Thompson 1931:342).

Le Plongeon's theatrics apparently convinced the workers that he was one of their great personages "disenchanted," and they agreed to continue their work, as well as pay homage. That his companion was a rifle toting woman, adept at using the somewhat mysterious surveying and photographic equipment, fluent in Maya, and sympathetic to their problems, no doubt contributed to the rapport the workers had with the Le Plongeons.

Such was the aura of mysticism growing around Le Plongeon that even simple coincidences became important events. One day Desiderio Kansal climbed the pyramid and entered the temple of Kukulcan, where he saw the bearded white one standing in front of an earthen vessel, "the kind the ancient ones used in burning incense before their gods" (Thompson 1931:342). In time such moments became part of the local lore and were passed down from father to son. Le Plongeon himself publicized such events, adding to the

reputation that was growing in Merida because of his "meditative" approach to finding the Chacmool.

The profile incident may have helped the Le Plongeons ward off hostile attacks from the Chan Santa Cruz. But publishing the episode brought no end of accusations and recriminations against him. Some stated that the whole story was a fabrication; others felt that it was true but was the product of a deranged mind.

The presence of the excavated Chacmool seemed to bring a mixture of danger and protection to the work at Chichen Itza. One day a Maya Cruzob guerrilla patrol came into the camp not only to pay homage but to see for themselves what the bearded white man was up to. Augustus had been warned by Colonel Felipe Díaz, commander of the troops covering the eastern frontier, that tracks of the hostile Maya had been discovered by his scouts. Díaz had advised them to keep a sharp look out, lest they be surprised by the enemy.

Several years later in *Vestiges of the Mayas,* his first book laying out his theories on the Maya, Augustus told the story of the encounter. "Now to be on the look out in the midst of a thick, well-nigh impenetrable forest," he wrote,

> is rather a difficult thing to do, particularly with only a few men, and where there is no road; yet all being a road for the enemy. Warning my men that danger was near, and to keep their loaded rifles at hand, we continued our work as usual, leaving the rest to destiny (1881a:55).

Suddenly and noiselessly the group appeared, emerging from the thicket, one by one. Realizing that the intruders were armed only with machetes, Le Plongeon ordered his

This bearded bas-relief figure on a capital atop the north side of El Castillo was of particular interest to the Le Plongeons, for they felt it supported Maya connections with the Old World. Philipp Valentini, a scholarly rival of Le Plongeon's, claimed in an article published by the American Antiquarian Society that the beard on this figure, and another on a figure in the North Temple of the Ball Court, were faked by Le Plongeon. Art historians have since agreed with Le Plongeon's findings that the beards are authentic and may represent ethnic peoples of Mexico and Yucatan. Stereo, 1875.

39

men not to shoot. Their leader was an old gray haired man, his eyes blue with age.

> He would not come near the statue, but stood at a distance as if awe-struck, hat in hand, looking at it. After a long time he broke out, speaking to his own people: "This, boys, is one of the great men we speak to you about." Then the young men came forward, with great respect kneeled at the feet of the statue, and pressed their lips against them.

Putting down his weapon, Augustus approached the old man and, offering his arm, led the Maya leader up the steep and crumbling stairs of El Castillo. When Augustus again placed his face next to the stone profile, the stranger fell on his knees and kissed his hand.

Then the old man, with a respectful but steady gaze began to ask Augustus if he remembered what happened while he was enchanted. It was quite a difficult question for Augustus to answer. It had to be a "correct" answer to retain his superior position, yet he did not know how many people might be hidden in the thicket. He compared being enchanted to a dream state that cannot be clearly recalled. "Well, father," Augustus concluded, "so it happened with me. I do not remember what took place during the time I was enchanted."

Satisfied with this answer, the Maya patrol went their way. Augustus wished them God-speed, and warned them not to go too near the villages on their way back to their homes, as people were aware of their presence in the country. "Whence they came, I ignore; and where they went, I don't know," Augustus concluded.

The Cruzob did not stay long that time, but the tension continued for the Le Plongeons and their workers. They must have wondered what would be the next step for the Maya after they paid homage to the Chacmool.

⊓ ⊓ ⊓

By January 1876 the Le Plongeons had moved the Chacmool to Piste. Their work at Chichen Itza came to an abrupt halt when Augustus was ordered to disarm his men, forcing them to retreat from Chichen Itza and Piste. There had been a revolt led by Theodosio Canto of those Maya allied with the Mexican government. It was feared the revolt would spread to other Maya soldiers in Yucatan; thus, the order was given to disarm all Maya soldiers, including Le Plongeon's small detachment. No amount of reassurances by Le Plongeon about his workers' loyalty could change the order.

Augustus described how they concealed the heavy statue, which they moved on a wheeled platform.

> At about a quarter of a mile from Piste, that is to say, far enough to put it out of the reach of mischief from the soldiers of the post, I placed it in a thicket about fifty yards from the road. There, with the help of Mrs. Le Plongeon, I wrapped it in oil-cloth and carefully closed the boughs on the passage that led from the road to the place of concealment, so that a casual traveller, ignorant of the existence of such an object, would not even suspect it (Salisbury 1877:97).

With the Chacmool hidden Augustus and Alice returned to the safety of Merida, where he wrote a letter to President Tejada, asking that they be allowed to exhibit the Chacmool in Philadelphia at the American Centennial Exposition. He also requested that he be included on a committee of Mexican scientists to accompany the exhibit and that there be made space available to him in the Mexican section of the exposition to display his finds. And he asked for presidential authorization to continue his investigations, with armed protection where needed. He did not intend to let local authorities halt the important work he and Alice were doing, just when they had made what they considered to be a significant breakthrough.

The Chaacmol arrived in Piste on a hand-hewn cart over a trail cut through a kilometer of jungle. Alice and an unidentified woman stand behind it, with the ruined church in the background, 1875. Stereo.

While they awaited a response from Mexico City, the Le Plongeons busied themselves in and around Merida. They wanted to be ready to travel with the Chacmool when they

41

received authorization from President Tejada. Their wait dragged on for months. To pass the time they traveled from one village to another in the vicinity, photographing Maya people and the ruined buildings of their ancestors.

They returned briefly to Uxmal to inspect some of the figures carved in relief on the beautiful limestone buildings. They wanted to look at the iconography in light of their new discoveries at Chichen Itza. It was a short visit, just long enough to persuade them that Queen Móo and other supposedly historic Maya figures they had seen at Chichen Itza were indeed pictured at Uxmal, too.

They were also drawn to the colonial towns of Motul and Ake. Like so many other Maya villages, their history stretched back into the days before the Spaniards came. Blending in with the sixteenth-century vaulted churches and the ubiquitous ellipsoidal thatched huts were limestone and stucco remains of more glorious days. The impressive, life-like stucco figures on the ancient walls at Ake were promising photographic material, but after only eight days the Le Plongeons were forced to leave because Alice was suffering from malaria. They withdrew to Tixkokob with the photographs and plans of the principal buildings, "regretting not to perfect our work by a complete survey of the whole of them, scattered as they are over a large extent of ground" (Salisbury 1877:100).

Meanwhile Tejada's answer finally came. Citing an 1827 law banning the export of artifacts, the president decreed that the Chacmool was not to be moved and could not be shown at the American Exposition.

Disappointed, Le Plongeon instead sent a few small artifacts and some photographs for display at the exposition. He could only hope that they might arouse the interest of the American people in Maya civilization. A swell of public sentiment might ease the bureaucratic problems that were beginning and might bring financial support as well. Feeling it was out of his hands for the moment, he and Alice made plans to travel to Isla Mujeres, and other islands on the east coast of the Yucatan peninsula.

They were unaware that bad luck plagued even the modest selection of artifacts and photographs sent to the exposition. They did not arrive in time, and, instead, were purchased by Stephen Salisbury for the American Antiquarian Society. The photographs, showing Alice and Augustus Le Plongeons' work at Uxmal, Chichen Itza, and Ake, as well as scenes of the Maya people of Yucatan, were pasted on display boards and titled "From the Wilds of Yucatan." With no fanfare and little explanation available for their interpretation, they had no apparent impact on American public opinion.

Meanwhile whatever alternate plans President Tejada may have had for the Chacmool were forgotten in the political turmoil of Mexico City. General Porfirio Díaz forced him to resign the presidency, and it would be months before Díaz's interest in the statue was to become clear.

Chapter 6

Along the Coast

The inhabitants are, as a general thing, a fine set of people. The men, mostly of Indian race, speaking among themselves the Maya language, are sinewy and athletic. They forcibly recalled to our minds the figures of warriors so beautifully portrayed on the walls of the inner room in the Chaacmol monument at Chichen Itza.—Augustus Le Plongeon in "Terra Cotta figure from Isla Mujeres" (Salisbury 1878:78)

Unaware of the problem befalling the artifacts sent to the United States and desiring to see new sites after their disappointment over the Chacmool, the Le Plongeons set sail for Isla Mujeres. They sailed round the north coast of Yucatan in a twenty-ton sloop called the *Viva*. Augustus found the nine-day trip tolerable. "All things considered—putting aside discomfort, danger of capsizing, and all other small inconveniences that we have become accustomed to bear patiently we did not fare as bad as we expected" (1876).

Alice did not fare as well during the first rough days of their voyage, as she confided daily to her diary:

21. At dusk anchored a short distance from land at a place called Telchac. How stupid I was to come in this miserable boat! 22. Stopped at Sacrisan, and again at Hocum. Don't know why. 23. Stopped at Dzilan. Wish the water would stop. Head wind.

Heavy thunderstorm. Very rough. Extra sick. Wish I
was dead! 24. Stopped at Holbox. Feel a little
better. Ate a cracker. Fine weather.

When she later published an account of the trip, she added,
"To those who have been seasick I need offer no apology for
such a diary; they will fully understand that I am not responsible" (1886a:2).

Arriving at Isla Mujeres, the *Viva* anchored in the Bay
of Dolores. Alice and Augustus began their search for ruins.

They first sought the Maya city of Ecab which, according to the Spanish historian Diego López de Cogolludo, was
on the mainland west of Isla Mujeres. It was said to be a
large city, inhabited even at the time of the conquest, although no recent travelers had mentioned it. They used their
spyglass, keeping a safe distance offshore, for the Quintana
Roo mainland was "territory of hostile Indians who without
asking if they like it or not, invariably kill every white individual who dares to indulge for a stroll on their premises."

Despite the danger and considerable inconvenience the
Maya hostilities caused, the Le Plongeons remained sympathetic to their position. Augustus wrote to a friend:

> Customs are said to change with time—when
> Spaniards first landed there, those people were very
> kind, welcomed them with open arms and doors—
> but since then, the conquerors and their
> descendants having made themselves obnoxious to
> the people—these in turn have changed their mild
> habits and acquired the strange custom of cutting
> any intruder to pieces (1876).

To explore Isla Mujeres Augustus hired a boat to sail
along the coast, searching for ruins. Local residents watched
them warily. The island had been used for years as a pirate's
lair, so they thought Alice and Augustus were on a treasure
hunt. Sailing down the west side of the island toward the
south point, they soon came upon a small destroyed structure. They were told that the walls still stood in 1848, "but
were demolished by the people who immigrated at that time,
in order to procure materials for building their houses" (Salisbury 1878:80). Then, on the narrowest part of the point,
they found what they guessed to be the main temple on the
island. They recorded a description of the structure and drew
a plan, showing a low-doored limestone room atop a square
platform with steps facing the shore.

A few days later Señor Don Salustino Castro, who lived
on the island of Cozumel, invited them along on a family
outing to see the ruins on Isla Mujeres. It was a welcome

invitation, and a chance for the Le Plongeons to explore the south end of the island again. On this visit to the temple Augustus noted a spot at the foot of the altar that had been disturbed. When one of Don Salustino's servants began shoveling in the soft sand, he unearthed a clay foot in a sandal. To Le Plongeon's dismay it had "unmistakable marks of having been just amputated from its corresponding leg."

Feeling very proud of his exploit, the servant was about to continue excavating when Augustus interceded.

> Falling on my knees, in presence of all the
> picnicking party, with my own hands, I carefully
> removed the damp sand from around an incense
> burner, of which the whole body of a female in a
> squatting posture had occupied the front part. It
> had lain there for ages, but alas! it was now before
> us in pieces (Salisbury 1878:83).

⊓ ⊓ ⊓

In other explorations on the coast of the peninsula the Le Plongeons inspected several sites of ruins. At El Meco, possibly also known as Ecab, they found remains of a stone construction,

> a ruined edifice surrounded by a wall forming an
> inclosure, adorned with rows of small columns. In
> the center of the inclosure an altar. The edifice,
> composed of two rooms, is built on a graduated
> pyramid composed of seven andenes [platforms].
> This building is without a doubt an ancient temple
> (Salisbury 1877:103).

They found similar structures at a place called Niscute and surmised that these small structures had been built by a race of small people, or dwarfs. They had heard numerous tales of *Aluxob,* a magical race of small people said to be living in the jungles of Yucatan, and knew there was a tradition of "little people" among the Maya, so they concluded the small buildings were the work of these same diminutive persons.[1]

As they made their way down the coast Augustus and Alice held out the hope of visiting the abandoned Maya city of Tulum, whose gleaming white walls on the rocky cliffs had so impressed the Spanish conquistadors when they first caught sight of it from their ships in 1519. But there were many Cruzob Maya in the village of Tulum, about three miles from the ruins. This was undisputedly their territory; Chan Santa Cruz, their headquarters, lay a dozen miles south connected by paths through the thick forest.[2] The Maya regularly burned copal incense and wax candles on the steps

47

of the ancient temples and practiced their ancestral religion. The village itself was a stronghold of the Speaking Cross oracle. A speaker hidden behind it gave prophesies and orders to the faithful to rally support for the Maya rebellion.

In Tulum María Uicab, a priestess, was said to evoke the power of the Cross, and in effect controlled the village. She had ordered the execution of a missionary who had landed near the village. Le Plongeon wanted badly to visit Tulum but knew that he did not have enough protection to hazard such a trip. "It is as much as one's life is worth to land at Tulum; the natives being hostile, make it necessary to be always on the alert and ready to take to the boat or fight," wrote Alice (1886a:66).

By early February 1877, realizing that the visit to Tulum was an impossibility, the Le Plongeons decided to explore Isla Cozumel, just off the coast a few miles north of Tulum. Upon landing at San Miguel, a scattered village of five hundred inhabitants, they requested a house, since they had no tent and planned to stay on the island for several months. After some delay they were grudgingly offered a dirty thatch-roofed room at the southeast corner of the immense grassy square that was the town plaza.

In their windowless hut they could see dry coconuts strewn about the damp floor and a pile of them in one corner, to which they immediately began adding others. "We were throwing one after another as fast as possible when the old priest of the village introduced himself and said he was glad to find out what the noise was, and he had feared it might be an earthquake coming on; though they had never had one in Cozumel" (1886a:28–29). The priest, Father Rejón, apologized for appearing in his shirtsleeves, explaining "I cannot afford to wear a coat everyday." He invited them to play cards with him in the evening "and also gave us the welcome intelligence that our house was haunted."

During the course of their days in San Miguel, the Le Plongeons heard many stories of local beliefs and customs. Father Rejón had lived there long enough that he himself had come to accept some of them, including the villagers' belief that he suffered from the evil eye, by which he could harm anything he looked at. Residents often accused him of such nefarious deeds as looking at a pig and causing it to drop dead, at which time they would of course ask him for remuneration. The poor curate could do little about the affliction and was convinced of its authenticity. The *padre* also knew of interesting ruins and natural formations on Cozumel. He happily offered to take the Le Plongeons around to explore the sites. On one such outing, they examined a small structure about a mile from the village, similar to others they had seen along the coast. Its doors, noted Augustus, were only three feet high and twenty inches wide.

Not far from the building Father Rejón showed them a cenote, somewhat obscured by a heavy growth of brush. To get a better look into the deep limestone sinkhole Augustus leaned out over the edge hanging onto a branch. Suddenly the branch broke, and he plummeted to the rocks below. He suffered a severe gash on his forehead, which bled profusely. Alice quickly scrambled down to him, but she could not control the bleeding even with a handkerchief held tightly over it. So she and one of the Maya assistants clambered down below to fill a gourd with cold water to help stop the bleeding. Try as she might she could not reach the water—two inches more and she could have filled the gourd.

Meanwhile Augustus was bleeding dangerously. His cut ran from the top of his forehead to the eyebrow, revealing the bone. Alice's Maya companion would not help her, apparently feeling the water to be sacred or thinking that the wound was beyond curing, so in desperation she drew her revolver and ordered the Maya to fill the gourd. He complied.

The wet handkerchief slowed the bleeding enough for her to lead her injured husband under the scorching sun back to their cottage. "Then I played the surgeon," Alice wrote. "Certainly the patient was much to be pitied in my hands; nor did I like the business. It was a jagged wound; bled for six hours, in spite of perchloride of iron, and refused to close by first intention" (1886a:51). The wound was slow to heal and caused a problem for some time. "After a new skin formed, I had to cut it to extract splinters that worked their way to the surface, though we believed they had all been washed out."

⊓ ⊓ ⊓

While the Le Plongeons coped with their problems on Cozumel, an armed force led by Juan Peón Contreras, director of the Museo Yucateco, marched out of Merida to retrieve the Chacmool. They cut a road through the jungle, and with the help of "150 indians," pulled the great statue on its wagon to Merida. There was great excitement in the capital over the arrival of the Chacmool, and a holiday was declared. A procession of dignitaries accompanied the statue into the city as a military band played.

The arrival of Le Plongeon's Chacmool at the capital was heralded as forming "an epoch in the annals of Yucatecan history" (*Periódico Oficial* 1877). But the politics of the moment completely overshadowed the discoverer of the statue. Even the dedication on its pedestal was changed from "the discovery of the wise archaeologist, Mr. Le Plongeon, in the ruins of Chichen Itza" (Salisbury 1877:95), to an exaltation of President Díaz and Governor Guerra for enriching the museum with such a priceless jewel.

The politicians of Yucatan had their time of glory, but it was short. A mere two months later, Señor Contreras was shocked to learn that the new Provisional Governor del Rio had given in to pressure from Mexico City, allowing the Chacmool to be carried off to the national museum. Federal troops loaded the statue aboard the war steamer *Libertad* and sailed to Veracruz. From there it went overland to the Department of State in Mexico City to be displayed at the national museum. Governor Guerra soon requested of President Díaz that a copy be sent to Merida as compensation.

When the news finally reached Cozumel that Governor Guerra had ordered the Chacmool and other pieces found by the Le Plongeons to be taken from Piste, Augustus sent a letter protesting the action. He appealed to the governor and the president to acknowledge his and Alice's ownership of the statue and other sculptured stones they had uncovered.

The 1827 law that President Tejada had used some months earlier to ban the exportation of the Le Plongeons' finds to the Centennial Exposition did not forbid the ownership of antiquities by private individuals. Le Plongeon therefore felt he should at least receive some redress for the amount of money and labor it took to uncover the Chacmool. And, as he pointed out, they had found the piece in disputed territory. At that time, Chichen Itza was not under control of the Mexican or Yucatecan governments, but in rebel territory. Furthermore, a law of Yucatan specifically stated that objects of value for the sciences and arts could be purchased at a just price from the finder, essentially acknowledging individual ownership of the object.

Le Plongeon next appealed, without success, to John W. Foster, the American ambassador in Mexico City, and A. J. Lespinasse, the American consul in Merida. Lespinasse did not want to become entangled in the affair, telling Le Plongeon that it is "a personal question between yourself and the parties who took possession of the statue" (1877).

The great pain the confiscation of their prize inflicted on the Le Plongeons was evident in a letter Alice wrote on April 3, 1877 to her friend Mrs. Gaylord.

> We have suffered from extreme indignation and
> sorrow, and have been quite unwell in consequence

of what has happened. The bust and most beautiful
fruit of our knowledge, labor, suffering, and heavy
expenditures, stolen: and by the Government of the
place where in we have made those expenses.

She recounted the hardships they had willingly endured,
depriving themselves

of all that makes life pleasant, and even of its
commonest necessities, in order to complete our
grand discovery. We have been sick to death in
places where we could not procure medicine of any
description, where, at times, we had not even bread;
and when we could obtain a few black beans or
some squash it was a feast.

Alice told Mrs. Gaylord of the perils of working in what
amounted to a war zone. "Surrounded by enemies, Remington always at hand, death lurking for us in every direction. All this was nothing, for we were buoyed up with the
pleasant thought of carrying Chacmool back to the world."

In September 1877 and again in April 1878 Augustus
wrote directly to President Díaz, petitioning for return of
the Chacmool, explaining carefully his legal position and
the amount of money and time he had expended in excavating it. Stephen Salisbury was asked to intercede through
his Washington connections. Senator George Hoar of Mas-
sachusetts presented Le Plongeon's claims to the United States
Congress in 1878, but no action was taken.

The matter was closed. The Chacmool was in Mexico
City and there it would remain. The Le Plongeons were to
receive no compensation.

Chapter 7

Looking for Sponsors

*After four years of toil and exposure to danger, and after a large
expenditure of money paid for services in opening roads, clearing
ruins, and making excavations, Dr. Le Plongeon finds himself
deprived of all the material results of his labors and sacrifices which
could secure him an adequate return.—Stephen Salisbury in "Dr. Le
Plongeon in Yucatan"* (Proceedings of the American Antiquarian
Society, 1877:108)

Dejected by their rebuff from the Mexican government,
the Le Plongeons decided to head farther south to British Honduras. In early 1878 they set sail from Cozumel
aboard a dilapidated twelve-ton schooner. It was captained
by a smuggler known as Antonio, "as unclean a specimen
of the Spanish sailor as we have ever had the misfortune to
see" (1886a:66–72).

On the first night out, Alice had to share the boat's tiny
cabin with the resident cockroach colony and a shipment
of turtles. She was suffering from a severe cold. "From a
second troubled doze upon my turtle pillow I was awakened
by a shout and, going to the foot of the scuttle, saw my
husband holding the tiller, giving orders in not sweet Spanish."

Roused by the sound of breakers only a few yards
ahead, he had found the helmsman fast asleep and was barely

"Business street in Belize [City]," 1878. The Le Plongeons were soon the center of attention among the British colonists. This may be one of the earliest photographs of Belize City.

able to veer the boat away from disaster. In the dark they could not be sure of their course.

> Not even a star glimmered overhead; we therefore went back about half a mile and hove to till morning. Daylight showed that we were entirely out of our course, and had been close upon the reefs at the entrance of Ascension Bay, where the water is very deep and alive with sharks.

Ascension Bay was but a few miles from the capital of the Cruzob at Chan Santa Cruz. To land on any part of the coast would have meant certain death. The hapless boat finally arrived in Belize City but waited offshore until after dark to allow Antonio to smuggle in a few thousand cigars to the local tobacconist.

Once on land the Le Plongeons began exploring the British colony. The abundance of Englishmen in government and lumber company positions gave them a new audience for their Yucatan adventures. Among those who were fascinated by the stories were Governor Henry Fowler, Lieutenant Governor Frederick Barlee, and Chief Justice William

A. Parker. They became lifelong friends of the Le Plongeons.

Several of the notables of the colony persuaded Alice to give a lecture on Yucatan as a fund raiser for a local Catholic school. The lecture, publicized as "Notes on Yucatan," illustrated by Augustus's photos, raised a good sum of money for the school. Alice sent the text of the lecture to Stephen Salisbury, who published it in the *Proceedings of the American Antiquarian Society* the next year.

Augustus was quite happy that Salisbury was taking his advice about publishing Alice's work as well as his own. In several previous letters to Salisbury, he had been emphatic about Alice's role and the credit she should receive. "Please do not forget that the scientific world is as much indebted to Mrs. Le Plongeon as to myself and that I decline receiving all the honors and see her deprived of her part she so richly deserves. So be kind enough not to publish my portrait unless hers is also published" (1877b).

The Le Plongeons spent four months exploring the ruins of northern British Honduras and even attempted to see the sites further north in Quintana Roo near Bacalar. They petitioned Crescencio Poot, leader of the Cruzob, for permission to enter their territory. They hoped that word of their sincere interest in the Maya might have reached him. Reach him or not, the Maya general was unmoved.

Instead they planned a visit to the site of Copan in

This expedition group with British officers may have accompanied the Le Plongeons during their exploration of northern British Honduras. The Maya load bearers may be from families who fled south to escape the War of the Castes, 1878. Stereo.

55

Honduras, which Augustus had been hoping to see since marvelling at Catherwood's drawings of the elaborately carved stelae there. They met with a Honduran general, Don Luís Bográn, and acquired a number of small artifacts from the excavation. The pieces were later deposited at the American Antiquarian Society.

By this time, the Le Plongeons were beginning to suffer financial difficulties, and things would not improve for them in the years to follow.

In 1878 Augustus wrote to Stephen Salisbury, "I have taken more views of Belize, in order to dispose of them here and pay our daily expenses." A new friend, Mr. Benar, was asked to help find a buyer for some of their pictures in London, and was given a letter of introduction to Alice's father, Henry Dixon. It could not hurt for Mr. Dixon to be given a first-hand account of his daughter's accomplishments and perhaps be nudged to lend some support.

In another letter to Salisbury Augustus thanked him for all the assistance he had given them in their efforts to publicize their research. He added that they were very short of funds and were prevented from doing anything further, unsupported as they were by any private or public institutions.

Augustus also suggested to Salisbury that he contact United States President Rutherford B. Hayes to see if Hayes could convince the Mexican government to provide armed protection for the Le Plongeons to return to Chichen Itza. Augustus provided the scenario. Salisbury would tantalize Hayes with the knowledge of a hidden cache of important sculptures whose whereabouts were known only to Le Plongeon. Anyone who assisted Augustus in presenting them to the world would gain great renown. Their reputation might rival Heinrich Schliemann, who excavated Troy, or General Luigi Palma de Cesnola, director of the Metropolitan Museum of Art who amassed a great collection of art objects.

In that same letter to Salisbury, Augustus brought up another issue that had haunted him since the early 1860s in Peru—the unauthorized publication of research findings and photographs by Ephraim G. Squier. Augustus had just received a copy of an article published by Squier in the February 1877 edition of *Harpers New Monthly Magazine*. The article contained several pages of photographs taken from Le Plongeon's glass plates.

Augustus had known since he first brought Alice to New York that Squier had illegally claimed ownership, but it was especially irksome that the problem surfaced again just after the Chacmool incident. And furthermore, Squier's only mention of Le Plongeon in reference to mapping and photographing the Peruvian sites was that he, Squier, was "accompanied by a friend who was both a draftsman and photographer," a "Mr. P." (McElroy 1977:737).

Augustus leveled another charge against Squier in his letter to Salibury. He accused Squier of robbing "Mrs. Centano's collection—keys of which had been entrusted to him as a gentleman by that lady—of the celebrated parietal bone on which a trepan operation had been performed." According to Augustus Squier gained some fame for presenting the Peruvian bone to the New York Ethnological Society and to specialists in Paris whose opinions were later published in the proceedings of the society. The bone, according to Le Plongeon, was retrieved from Squier by a member of the diplomatic corps and returned to Mrs. Centano.

The analysis Augustus made of Squier's research methods was direct and blunt, following the pattern he used throughout his life when attacking opponents. He told Salisbury that Squier had little to contribute to scientific research and that observation of him in the field led to the opinion

> that he is a most unscrupulous and superficial man. I have not read his last work on Peru (he might at least send me a copy in part payment for my negatives)—but I feel certain that many pages are mere plagiarism, as we find in his book on Nicaragua.

Squier's apparent successful use of the photographs from Peru became even more exasperating as the Le Plongeons' financial situation worsened. By now Augustus had expended the money acquired from California land dealings and from the Peruvian ventures in photography, publishing, and his medical clinic. The expenditures for travel, living, and the payment of Maya workers were great, even by the standards of the day. It was becoming clear that it was time to actively look for sponsors.

In 1879 *The Nation* carried a letter to the editor which discussed Augustus Le Plongeon's work. It was signed "A.D." (Alice Dixon perhaps). It suggested that the "courageous hard-working, enthusiastic field archaeologist" be given financial support.

In April 1880 the Le Plongeons returned to New York to secure political and monetary support. By all accounts they were successful. Pierre Lorillard, a well-known cigarette manufacturer, provided some financial backing. After discussions about their research, Stephen Salisbury arranged meetings in Washington with United States Secretary of State S. M. Everts.

Supreme Court Justice Stephen Field, an old friend of Augustus from his gold rush days in Marysville, also applied his influence in Washington. The outcome of the meeting with Everts was his agreement to see that Augustus got permits to work again in Yucatan. The resulting intercession of the new American ambassador, Judge Phillip Morgan, paved the way for the Le Plongeons to receive Porfirio Díaz's blessing to continue their work in Yucatan. The one compromise they were asked to make was to drop all claims to the Chacmool. Everts, Morgan, and Salisbury made it clear to Augustus that he could make fine progress in Mexico once that issue was settled.

The Le Plongeons also became acquainted with General Cesnola of the Metropolitan Museum of Art, who requested that Augustus make casts of his molds for an exhibit at the museum. Since such an exhibit could lead to purchase of the entire collection, the Le Plongeons reasoned, they readily agreed to the proposal, even though preparation of the casts would cost them a sizeable sum in advance. These molds and accompanying photographs of Uxmal were delivered to General Cesnola before Alice and Augustus returned to Yucatan, with the understanding that the casts would be made under his direction.

Shortly before his departure from New York Lorillard discussed the possibility of an exploration of Tulum with Augustus. As Augustus explained, the political circumstances made it impossible. Somewhat displeased and suffering from gout, Lorillard agreed to more limited objectives and provided money. Six years later when Augustus published his second major work on the Maya, *Sacred Mysteries Among the Mayas and Quiches, 11,500 Years Ago,* he dedicated it to Lorillard in gratitude for his assistance.

The Le Plongeons' three months in New York were a welcome break from Yucatan. Despite the many meetings and interviews about money, they renewed old friendships and enjoyed a whirlwind of social events. But when the promise of assistance was in hand, they were ready to return to the fieldwork they loved. They left New York on July 1, 1880 bound for Yucatan.

After eight days at sea they landed in Progreso and soon traveled to Mexico City, via Veracruz, at the request of Judge Morgan to discuss their research plans in Yucatan. According to Augustus Judge Morgan was "a perfect gentleman in every sense of the word" (1880a). On September 25, Augustus went to his first meeting with President Díaz, escorted by the judge. Augustus was well pleased with the reception the President gave them. "He received us, I must say with opened

French photographer and explorer Désiré Charnay, 1826–1915. Le Plongeon despised what he considered Charnay's elitist attitude toward the Maya and considered his photographic and ethnographic work to be of an inferior nature. Le Plongeon threatened to give him the "cold shoulder" should he run into him in Yucatan. Etching, "On the March," from Charnay's Ancient Cities of the New World, *1887.*

arms, and appeared gratified that I should have come to Mexico and have paid my respects to him. I told him what I wanted from the Mexican government" (1880a).

Augustus requested permission to excavate the ruined monuments of Yucatan and make molds of the inscriptions and bas-reliefs they found. As Augustus told it General Díaz was impressed that the archaeologist would ask for "so little." He readily gave permission to export the molds. And he promised, "All objects that you may find underground will be yours provided you leave a small part for our museum" (1880a).

Near the end of October Alice and Augustus again met President Díaz, this time socially at his home. "Then and there," Augustus wrote to Stephen Salisbury, "he repeated his offers spontaneously made in the presence of the American Minister" (1880b).

Before the Le Plongeons left Mexico City to return to Yucatan, Augustus gave several lectures at the National Museum, and made a cast from the head of the Chacmool which was now displayed in a prominent spot at the museum. They were also feted by the diplomatic corps and prominent members of the American community over the course of several months. On one such occasion Judge Morgan gave a ball in honor of Alice. The Le Plongeons arrived late, because Alice, "with the help of her lady friends," had to fix one of her dresses for the occasion. When they finally arrived, around 10 P.M., Judge Morgan began introducing them to his guests. One guest invited to meet Dr. Le Plongeon was Désiré Charnay. Judge Morgan supposed that Charnay would have much in common with Augustus.

When Charnay, who was conversing with a correspondent of The *New York World,* heard Augustus being introduced to someone behind him, he turned and asked him if he was indeed Dr. Le Plongeon. Apparently Charnay was not as thrilled with the meeting as the host had expected him to be. Augustus recalled, "On being answered in the affirmative, he soon rose and was seen no more in the ballroom or any where else in the legation during that night" (1880b). There were other times that their paths crossed, but Charnay always found an excuse to avoid Augustus. He was not a man of "manners and good breeding," Augustus concluded. This was only the beginning of a rivalry between the two that would go on for years.

Chapter 8

Now for the Facts

My duty, to the scientific world, is to keep entirely neutral towards all contending parties. I possess a great advantage. I study the monuments in situ. I hear from the mouth of the natives—in their mother tongue, the Maya—whatever they have learned from their ancestors of these monuments. My knowledge must, of necessity, be greater than that of gentlemen, who write from behind their desks, ignorant of the true facts.—Augustus Le Plongeon in "Mayapan and Maya inscriptions" (Proceedings of the American Antiquarian Society 1881b:249)

By November 1880 the Le Plongeons were back in Yucatan at the site of Mayapan, 30 miles from Merida, looking for keys to the undeciphered Maya hieroglyphic writing. It was their first visit to the site, and they enjoyed the monetary assistance of Pierre Lorillard and the hospitality of Don Vicente Solís de León, one of the owners of the Hacienda X-canchacan where Mayapan was located.

As one of his primary purposes at Mayapan, Augustus wanted to present the facts about Maya inscriptions. Several essays had appeared, including one by Professor Philipp J. J. Valentini, that seemed to dismiss a Maya alphabet, recorded just after the conquest, as a mere invention of the Bishop of Yucatan, Diego de Landa. Le Plongeon hoped to prove that the alphabet was authentic. His strategy was to straightforwardly report on the monuments and the knowledge of living Maya.

Using his knowledge of spoken Maya, Augustus intended to strengthen his argument that Landa's Maya alphabet was of some use in understanding Maya hieroglyphics. His premise was that the letters recorded by Landa's scribes were still in use at the time and probably corresponded to the glyphs carved in stone. Augustus reasoned that Landa must have believed the only way to disengage the Maya from old beliefs was to take away all of their books, which were the key to their religious beliefs and translatable only by those who understood the glyphs. Citing the Bishop's fervor in destroying all Maya books that fell into his hands, Augustus argued, "For I ask how can a reasonable and honest man deny that the probabilities are in favor of Landa?"

Augustus also hoped that he might find an inscription written in two or three languages, a sort of Rosetta Stone of the Maya. This was his first thought when he saw Stela One, called the Stela of Mayapan. As he studied the incised slab, he soon realized that even if it had once been a translatable text, they could no longer decipher its weathered carvings. He could make out enough details to write some comments about the iconography on the lower section of the stela. The floral design on the headdress reminded him of similar reliefs on the northeast end of the portico of the Castillo, and on the Lower Temple of the Jaguars at Chichen Itza. He believed it to be the *Cocom* flower, "a peculiar yellow flower, well known in the eastern and southern portions of the peninsula."

In the Maya dictionary of Don Pio Pérez, compiled earlier in the nineteenth century, he found the definitions of Cocom: "Cocom is a sarmentous plant [having runners], with yellow flowers. . . . Cocom was the name of an ancient Maya dynasty, and is still preserved as an Indian family name among the natives of Yucatan."

Le Plongeon found a passage in Landa's *Relación de las Cosas de Yucatán,* a book in which Landa recorded Maya stories about the gods and ancient ruling families that seemed to suggest that the individual on the stela was of the house of Cocom. Augustus concluded that the personage depicted on the stone monument was of great authority, possibly a king, because of his height on the stela relative to an accompanying figure. The lower figure was on a low stool to symbolize his inferiority.

In addition to analyzing the carving at Mayapan, Augustus surveyed some structures and determined the latitude of the site. Using this, he hypothesized that a large mound with two upright columns on top was used as an astronomical gnomon, or time indicator. The two columns provided a fixed point for gauging the sun's position.

In his report to the American Antiquarian Society, "Mayapan and Maya Inscriptions," Augustus used elaborate calculations based on his measurements of the gnomon mound to support the notion that it was used by Maya priests to observe the passage of time. He felt that the mound was built to keep track of the ritual 260-day, and the solar 365-day calendars.[1]

He stopped short of trying to explain *why* they had adopted two modes of computing time.

> Whatever be the theories presented to the world by
> others, my duty toward you, and towards the
> students of American Archaeology, is to present, on
> what I see; because I do not believe that we possess,
> as yet, sufficient positive and incontrovertible data
> for any one to form a true and correct opinion on
> the subject, free from hypothesis (1881b:272).

He compared the Maya understanding of the heavens to that of the Egyptians and Chaldeans. Augustus found it easier to say he would refrain from hypothesizing than to actually do it.

After surveying the pyramid of Kukulcan, the great plumed serpent, and other structures at Mayapan, Augustus designated them as "belonging to the latter period, in order to distinguish them from the most ancient (which are built of solid stone masonry from their foundations to their summits, as those of Khorsabad)" (1881b:275). Noting that the later buildings were not constructed with the care and precision of earlier Maya buildings, he assumed that the difference carried through to the core. Not having excavated the finely built structures of the classic Maya period, he did not realize they were also rubble filled.

口 口 口

At the close of his report to the American Antiquarian Society, Augustus cited Lorillard and Fred P. Barlee for their moral and material support of his and Alice's work in Yucatan. He thanked Senator George F. Hoar, vice president of the society, and Stephen Salisbury for their attempts "to induce the American Government to protect me as an American citizen abroad, and a scientist whose explorations were interrupted." He noted also the indifference of the American scientific societies, which were unwilling to support him through purchase of his photographs and tracings. Yet they "wanted to procure from me *gratis* what had cost me so much time, labor and money to acquire."

Le Plongeon was fed up by what he considered to be gross indifference on the part of the American scientific community. He hardened his resolve. "I made up my mind to keep my knowledge, so dearly purchased, to destroy some day or other my collections, and to let those who wish to know about the ancient cities of Yucatan, do what I have done."

Such neglect was not necessarily the case in other countries, he noted, citing entreaties by Barlee and various acquaintances in England that led the Le Plongeons to publish more of their research there, despite the unfavorable notice it often received.

> The main cause of my unwillingness to say more on
> the subject is, that my former writings, when
> published, have been so curtailed and clipped, to
> make them conform with certain opinions and ideas
> of others, that my own have altogether disappeared,
> or have been so disfigured as to cause me to be
> taken for what I am not—an enthusiastic theorist
> following in the wake of Brasseur de Bourbourg.

Before he left Mayapan, Le Plongeon had made casts of several carvings, which he sent to Lorillard as thanks for his financial assistance. Lorillard donated the casts to the American Antiquarian Society.

The Le Plongeons then returned to Uxmal for a few more weeks of research.

Chapter 9

Life in the Governor's Palace

We are settled for the present in what is called the "Governor's House." It is the most central building, and from its broad terraces we look upon all the surrounding monuments, which cover an immense extent of ground. Far beyond are the hills, the same that were gazed upon by the people who dwelt here so long ago.—Alice Le Plongeon in "Ruined Uxmal" (New York World, June 27, 1881)

By their third visit to Uxmal in June and July of 1881 Alice and Augustus knew what they were looking for. They had been studying their earlier photographs of the site, comparing iconographic details with those at Chichen Itza. Their goal was to complete the record and report the irrefutable results to the public through the American Antiquarian Society's *Proceedings,* as well as other books and newspaper articles, and public lectures.

They wanted to find every shred of evidence that supported their reconstruction of Maya history revolving around Queen Móo and Prince Coh. Based on the figures they had studied on the murals in the upper Temple of the Jaguars at Chichen Itza, they thought they saw Queen Móo's profile in a motif on the facade of the Governor's Palace. It was an unclear image, shadowy, not visible from every angle, and of uncertain origin. The Le Plongeons said it was carved

Augustus Le Plongeon found important evidence in this motif on the east facade, north wing, of the Governor's Palace in Uxmal. He interpreted an asymmetrical motif in the lower left corner as a profile of Queen Móo of Chichen Itza, 1881. 5 × 8 inch.

under the direction of Queen Móo's brother, Prince Aac. Their interpretation did little, in the end, to bolster their increasingly unpopular theory of Maya cultural diffusion and history. Augustus was accused of intentionally falsifying the photograph when he touched it up. He did highlight some details to clarify the profile, making it apparent to anyone looking at the photograph.

Augustus had an additional incentive for developing his arguments about very ancient connections between Egypt and the Maya; he also wanted to find the origin of Freemasonry, which many wanted to trace to Egypt. As a Mason himself Augustus knew the symbolism of that secret fraternal society and found what he considered to be ample evidence

Le Plongeon enlarged the detail he identified as Queen Móo's profile and added slight retouching, probably to help the untrained eye see the image. This supposed appearance at Uxmal would have supported Le Plongeon's argument that Queen Móo of Chichen Itza was indeed an important personage. It was later published in Queen Móo and The Egyptian Sphinx, *(plate LXV, 1896).*

of it at Uxmal. He concluded that the Maya must have been direct antecedents of those who founded Masonry. This would mean that its origins were more ancient than if it had begun in Egypt. The surest signs, he felt, were a skull and cross-bones carved on the Adivino Pyramid, and a sculptured torso with an inverted hand on an apron, both Masonic symbols.

Le Plongeon found Masonic symbolism in the fragment of a statue he found at Uxmal. After he showed the piece to two American friends in Merida it disappeared, leaving only his sketch which he published in an article for Harper's Weekly, *"An interesting discovery. A temple with Masonic symbols in the ruined city of Uxmal" (1881d).*

"At home in the Governor's Palace," commented Maude Blackwell when she saw this photo of her friends Augustus and Alice. They set up house-keeping in the central rooms, with hammock and mosquito netting hung in the inner room and dishes, including wine goblets, in the foreground. Field equipment—guns, butterfly net, surveyor's instrument, tripod and tape measure, and helmets—stand ready. The view camera sits behind Alice amid a pile of books on the table. Augustus writes field notes, with Trinity their dog napping at his feet. Photo was made by remote shutter release or by an assistant. Circa 1874. 5 × 8 inch.

Augustus showed the torso briefly to two Masonic friends in Merida. Then it disappeared, its fate shrouded in mystery. Without this piece to support the Freemasonry connection, a more cautious person might have dropped that line of reasoning, knowing it would be controversial. But Augustus persisted and even used certain architectural features, including the Maya corbelled arches, similar to ones used in Egypt, as further evidence of the connection.

During this last intensive period of research at Uxmal, the Le Plongeons set up housekeeping in the Governor's Palace stringing their hammocks in one of the raised inner rooms, while using the outside room as a spot for writing field notes. At the end of a hot, humid day of climbing up and down shaky scaffolding to expose one plate after another, they would retreat into the coolness of the Governor's Palace. There they could relax and discard their Remington rifles and pith helmets. With their dog Trinity at their feet, they would record insights of the day.

Their living room also served as their photographic studio and kitchen, complete with campfire, cooking pots, and storage flasks. There were few leisure activities beyond reading, writing, strumming the guitar, or napping in the safety of the mosquito-netted hammock. Alice amused herself by pondering the variety of creatures that shared their existence. "There is no solitude here, though far from the abodes of living men. The place swarms with life and perfect

silence never reigns, for every tiny insect has something to say for itself" (1881b:1–2).

Every creature seemed preoccupied with finding water, from iguanas who noisily prowled their room at night, to

> foolish bees which throw themselves into any liquid they can find and part with life for a drop of it. When they feel the dark waves closing over them they doubtless repent of the rash deed, and having taken a drink and a bath, are very grateful if anyone will ladle them out.

Worst of all, in Alice's opinion, were the blood-sucking flying bed bugs.

> When they began to feed on one it is like a needle running in the flesh. A dozen of them will give you bad dreams and draw an ounce of blood. Man does not require bleeding every night in a place where food is scarce and work plentiful.

Indeed, the effects of insect borne diseases, lack of supplies, and other characteristics of the tropical lowlands were beginning to show on Alice and Augustus. They merely had to look at each other to see how rapidly they were aging.

Nevertheless the tasks they assigned themselves in these later visits were no less strenuous than in earlier years. Their goal was to record the iconographic detail that would support the existence of the historical figures they had discovered at Chichen Itza. To do so they began with overall views of the Governor's Palace and other structures, then made

Alice sits in the center room of the Governor's Palace, waiting for the pot to boil. At the left is a water barrel; at the right, a covered gourd for carrying water. She wrote extensive descriptions of life in the Governor's Palace in a series of 1881 articles for The New York World. *Circa 1874. 5 × 8 inch.*

69

Augustus photographing the entire east facade of the Governor's Palace at Uxmal, circa 1873. The result was an undistorted panorama in sixteen stereo segments. Ladder was supported by a sapling buttress. Photograph by Alice Le Plongeon. 5 × 8 inch.

detailed and accurate plans of them. Their confidence that interpretation was possible relied on their basic assumption "that the human mind and human inclinations and wants are the same in all times, in all countries, in all races when civilized and cultured" (1881a:16). They also painstakingly studied and recorded the ornamental details that covered the upper registers of the buildings. Out of those complex patterns, they hoped to solve the riddle of their designs. Augustus wrote, "We believe that if a human intelligence had devised it, another human intelligence would certainly

be able to unravel it." But it was first necessary, they knew, to be intimately familiar with the inventory of what was there at Uxmal. And no one had yet taken the time, they felt, to do that adequately. Charnay certainly had not during his short visit.

Augustus photographed the entire 320-foot east facade of the Governor's Palace in sixteen overlapping stereo photos. Alice recorded him balancing on a ladder with his large view camera. For each photograph the process was the same. Each glass plate had to be sensitized in a bath of collodion silver nitrate solution, rushed up the ladder and to the camera to keep the plate from losing its sensitivity, exposed for a calculated amount of time, then rushed to the darkroom for development. Photographs of the Governor's Palace could be developed in the darkroom in their makeshift quarters. But work at other buildings not on the palace platform required a portable darkroom.

Augustus also made eighty-three molds of the Governor's Palace to record the low reliefs and other details too small or too difficult to photograph. Alice photographed him hard at work carefully forming the wet papier-maché onto the bas-reliefs.

The molds produced precise details and added new information not visible in the stereo photos. The craftsmanship of these three-dimensional replicas drew great praise. Louis Aymé, American consul in Merida, who later had violent conflicts with Le Plongeon, lauded his workmanship. He glowingly commented to Stephen Salisbury that Le Plongeon's "paper moulds are really exquisite." This provided encouragement for the Le Plongeons to continue the time-

Augustus made a photographic panorama of the 320-foot facade on the east side of the Governor's Palace in 16 stereo sections. Circa 1873. Segments of that panorama are shown on pages 71–73.

71

Augustus Le Plongeon on scaffold making molds of the center motif on the east facade of the Governor's Palace, Uxmal, circa 1873. Photograph by Alice Le Plongeon. 5 × 8 inch.

consuming project. They hoped to sell them to American museums to help finance their work in Yucatan. The possibility of presenting the Maya to the world through an impressive reconstruction of a temple facade at an international exhibition was also on their minds. For of what value was their work if it was not to reveal the greatness and antiquity of the Maya to an appreciative audience?

Alice recorded their observations. She wove some of them into vignettes about Yucatan which she sent back to New York to be published. The *New York World* carried several of her pieces. In one article on Uxmal Alice described the Governor's Palace, giving measurements of the rooms and the directions they face. She described the sequence of construction, surmising that the "wings" extending beyond the

Alice sitting in the south arch of the Governor's Palace, Uxmal, circa 1873. 5 × 8 inch.

corbelled arches were built at a later time because the stone work was inferior to the main sections. She identified vestiges of stone rings fastened in the inner part of the walls on each side of the entrance as curtain holders. Her experience with actually living in the rooms of the structure allowed her to comment on their comfort.

> It might be supposed that these chambers would be close and unhealthy. Far from it. They make delightful habitations, and their atmosphere is never oppressive. During the heat of day they are so cool that to step outside is like entering a heated oven, and at night, when the air is sometimes damp and chilly, they are comfortably warm (1881b:1–2).

Alice described the condition of the rooms, the thickness of the walls, and the destruction caused by a large hole dug by John L. Stephens into the west wall from inside the center room. She surmised that Stephens must have thought that a wall two meters, fifty centimeters thick must contain a room, though there was no trace whatever of a doorway.

Instead, Alice hypothesized, at the more ancient time it was built, "cyclones and other atmospheric disturbances may have made it necessary thus to strengthen the structure in its lofty position."[1]

Alice was amused by the recent hiding of large phallic stones at the southeastern corner of the terrace on which the Governor's Palace stood.

> The round columns and the religious symbols they supported, which once stood on it, were thrown down by order of the owner of the hacienda, Don Simon Peon, at the time when the Empress Carlotta visited these ruins, lest she should be offended by the sight of them!

She also described vistas from the platform, and the difficulty of climbing the steps of the pyramidal structures at Uxmal.

> From afar is the Dwarf's House, on the summit of an artificial mound one hundred feet high. The ascent is . . . so perpendicular that some of those who go up, when they have to descend wonder how they could have been so rash, and repent having made the attempt (1885:376).

The steep structure, the Adivino Pyramid, was constructed in five phases, they determined, with the House of the Dwarf and other temples built in different styles highlighting various parts of the structure. Recording these phases was an important but extremely difficult task. From the roof of the adjacent Nunnery Quadrangle Augustus photographed an elaborately carved temple half way up the west side of the pyramid, using lenses of different focal lengths.

From a precarious ladder set near the edge of a fifty-foot drop-off on the structure itself he photographed the same temple close up. That room with its serpent-mouth doorway attracted him. Over the doorway hung a huge mask of the rain god Chac, its curling nose broken off. Above the nose, and barely visible without a ladder were two very interesting figures on their hands and knees. Covering the temple facade were a large number of carved motifs that Augustus attempted to interpret.

Augustus made forty-three molds of decorations from the temples on the Adivino Pyramid in order to preserve them and give himself and Alice research material. Making molds of small sculptures and architectural details was also a way to take momentos away from the site while not contributing to its destruction. This was important to the Le Plongeons who were appalled by the senseless destruction they were beginning to see. Alice condemned the actions of visitors who were already leaving graffiti on the walls of Uxmal and other sites in the 1870s and 1880s.

> The walls of the rooms are now covered with the
> names of visitors in letters of every size and color.
> Some silly people, called civilized, have thought
> theirs so important that they have painted them on
> several walls within the same building (1881a:2).

In addition to photographing the temples on the Adivino Pyramid, Augustus used the pyramid itself as a platform to make a stereopticon panorama of the site. The series of photographs, from the Governor's Palace to the Nunnery Quadrangle, presented an almost 180-degree perspective. No one had ever done anything quite like this before at

After setting up his ladder to photograph details of the Chenes Temple on the Adivino Pyramid, Augustus took this shot of Alice and their Maya assistant. He proceeded with the straight-on detail shots, oblivious to the precipitous drop just behind the ladder. Circa 1876. Stereo.

In this straight-on treatment of the East Building of the Nunnery Quadrangle, Augustus controlled his line of sight to keep the Adivino Pyramid from looming in the background. Circa 1873. 5 × 8 inch.

Uxmal. The Le Plongeons hoped that this near re-creation of this spectacular Maya city would cause quite a stir among those who doubted the greatness of the Maya.

Other views included a scene of the prehispanic ball-court lying in ruins between the terraces of the Governor's Palace and the Nunnery Quadrangle. Its two small low rectangular buildings formed the boundaries of the playing space. Alice measured and described what she called the tennis court for the *New York World*.

> Portions of two large stone rings, and fragments of stone pillars, with the feathers of the winged serpent carved on them, are on the ground. The rings were originally opposite each other, above the middle and near the top of the wall (1881c:2).

Recalling the writings of the seventeenth-century Spanish historian Fray Juan de Torquemada, she described the ball-game.

> The players were to receive the ball on the hip, and from there by a peculiar motion of the hip throw it upward. If they succeeded in throwing it through either of the rings, it was their right to seize the cloaks of as many of those present as they could catch.

The last major focus of the Le Plongeons' research at Uxmal was the Nunnery Quadrangle, the large four-structure complex to the west of the Adivino Pyramid. When they

first saw the complex, the east structure stood intact, having suffered little from eight hundred years of abandonment. However the west and north buildings were in need of major repairs.

Most of the facade on the West Building had fallen shortly before 1841, when Stephens and Catherwood were at the site. During that visit the hacienda owner Don Simón had told Stephens that "in 1835 the whole front stood, and the two serpents were seen encircling every ornament in the building" (1843:179). Don Simón's intention was to preserve one of the serpent heads in the wall of a house in Merida as a memorial of Uxmal. Beyond that, he told them, they could "tear out and carry away every other ornament."

By the time the Le Plongeons saw it, only a few sections of the West Building's upper register were left intact. However, Alice made special note of the intertwining feathered serpents of the west facade, so Don Simón must not have carried out his plan. But a large section of smooth facing stones from the lower register of the South Building had just been removed, and the limestone mortar had not even begun to weather.

The arch on the South Building had a large crack which gave it the appearance of being near collapse. Alice observed, "It begins at the base on one side, runs down again to the base on the opposite side. This is the consequence of the removal of the stone facing by means of crowbars" (1881c:2). She also noted traces of blue, yellow, and red paint and nine

In details such as this panel of Chac Masks from the north-west corner of the East Building of the Nunnery Quadrangle, Augustus showed his mastery of photography. He was proud of the sharpness and excellent tonal range he was able to achieve, even in less than ideal field conditions. Circa 1873. 5 × 8 inch.

79

red hand imprints on the arch, a feature not uncommon on the smooth stucco walls and ceilings of Maya rooms.

In 1860 Désiré Charnay had found the buildings in essentially the same condition. When he photographed them he had tried to compensate for distortion in low angle shots by adjusting the lens board of his view camera. Le Plongeon wanted to avoid all distortion in his photographs, so he built ladders for straight-on detail shots. He augmented these detailed photos with seventeen more molds from the Nunnery Quadrangle.

Alice's descriptions of the iconographic and architectural details at Uxmal also included hypotheses on water storage and population estimates. From practical experience she knew that the pronounced dry season would have made some form of community water management necessary. One reservoir she examined was on the north side of the Nunnery court.

> Our studies lead us to understand that they were built solely for the reception of rain water on which depended a population of 30,000 to 40,000 for they had to dig very far into the bowels of the earth to obtain even a small quantity otherwise (1881b:2).

She described the North Building facade as "very elaborate but by no means chaste," referring to more phallic symbolism that had escaped being torn down for the visit of Empress Carlotta.

A factor that must have made the Le Plongeons' final field season at Uxmal more difficult was publicity surrounding the discovery of a sculpture which they thought to be Chaacmol's brother. On June first, at the beginning of that visit, Augustus had made a mold of an inscription, which he gradually came to interpret as meaning Cay, the elder brother of Chaacmol. The thought struck him that an effigy of Cay might be hidden nearby in the buried lower part of the Adivino Pyramid. He tunneled into a wall and after three yards,

> I suddenly found myself in the presence of a superb cast of the personage whose name I was then satisfied I had interpreted rightly, since the diadem that adorned his brows sustained his totem—the head of a fish, Cay in the Maya language being a fish (Alice Le Plongeon 1881c:10).

Augustus was then visited by two members of the American community in Merida to whom he showed his find. He asked them to keep his discovery a secret, but one of the party indiscreetly leaked the news to a Merida newspaper,

much to Augustus's dismay. "From that day my position in Uxmal became, if possible, more annoying than before. The administrator of the plantation endeavored in every way to discover where I had found the bust of Chaacmol's brother."

The administrator's interests lay not only in Maya sculpture, but also in the finely polished limestone building blocks, which he intended to carry off for reuse. To stop this, Augustus had to devise a plan that would scare him and other would-be scavengers away from the site. He decided to spread the rumor that he had booby-trapped certain unspecified places there. He did this through a notice in the July 19 *Eco de Comercio* saying that he had placed dynamite near the monument. This published statement, though made to protect the monuments, brought harsh criticism to Le Plongeon.

Alice conceived of a way that might help spread the word of his innocence. She used a November 1881 *New York World* interview to explain his reported use of dynamite. In it, Alice the author asked Augustus the archaeologist, "Is it true that you put dynamite in monuments to protect them from Indians?" He recounted the origin of the story, explaining that he was trying to prevent destruction

> not at the hands of the Indians, who stand in awe
> of the effigies of the ancient rulers of the country,
> but by the very administrator who is destroying
> these monuments, by order of the master, to use the
> stones in the building of his farmhouse.

The dynamite ploy may have temporarily curbed some dismantling of the ancient Maya buildings, but Le Plongeon's name became inextricably linked with dynamite at Uxmal, and later at Chichen Itza, and would continue to serve as a rallying cry for those who wished to defame him.

Augustus points to a stone phallus which he has collected with other sculptural details near the southeast corner of the Nunnery Quadrangle, Uxmal. The Le Plongeons were amused that much of the phallic symbolism had been removed or hidden when the Empress Carlotta had visited the site a few years earlier. Photograph by Alice Le Plongeon. Circa 1881. Stereo.

81

Nevertheless, Augustus and Alice continually sought to make the deteriorating condition of the ruins known to the world. In another 1881 *New York World* article, Alice wrote,

> The Peninsula of Yucatan is strewn with fragments
> of departed grandeur; silent, deserted, fallen cities.
> Some are not approachable without danger, lying as
> they do within the territories of hostile tribes.
> Others—and these are the worst treated—are in the
> power of the whites.

Laws to protect the antiquities of Mexico were difficult to enforce. Warfare and disease contributed to the turbulent political atmosphere. Augustus deplored the destruction of Uxmal by the owner of the hacienda and threatened to call in government officers to try to stop what he described as the "fury for destruction of the handiwork of the ancient inhabitants of this peninsula" (Augustus Le Plongeon 1881c). Yet in his heart he doubted that even government officials could stop the tide of destruction.

Chapter 10

Less-than-Professional Feuds

"Still we cannot refrain from expressing the regret that Dr. Le Plongeon's enthusiasm is so apparent in his reports, a judicial frame of mind, as well as the calmness which accompanies it, are requisite both for scientific work and the inspiration of confidence in the reader." *Thanks for the advice! Who is to know best, Mr. Short, who has never seen [the ruins], or Dr. Le Plongeon, who has made a special study of them,* in situ, *during seven years?—Augustus Le Plongeon quoting author John T. Short in a footnote to "Mayapan and Maya inscriptions"* (Proceedings of the American Antiquarian Society, *1881b:282*)

In October 1881 Alice and Augustus left Uxmal, vowing to return to finish their research if they could raise enough money. They traveled to New York, expecting to have realized a profit from exhibition of the casts of their Uxmal molds at the Metropolitan Museum of Art. Instead they discovered that General Cesnola had not only failed to exhibit the pieces, but had also mishandled them. The Le Plongeons found the casts in the basement of the museum, many of them broken. Alice and Augustus were distressed by the apparent lack of concern shown for their work and were further appalled by the museum director's attitude. "General Cesnola greatly resented our chagrin and never forgave us for expressing it, although our remarks were more than moderate and self contained" (Alice Le Plongeon 1900a).

Though the opportunity to exhibit at the Metropolitan and to sell the casts was lost, Augustus did exhibit his photos at the American Archaeological Exhibition in Madrid. That and arranging for the publication of his first book on ancient civilizations, *Vestiges of the Mayas,* were two bright spots in this less than successful fund-raising trip. The book was Augustus's first major statement of his conclusions. It was an outline of the central points on diffusionism he would argue for the next twenty years.

Meanwhile Augustus's friendship with Stephen Salisbury began to be strained and the interest of the American Antiquarian Society in the Le Plongeons' research began to cool. In fact, it appeared that individuals in the society were trying to isolate him. Feeling that his patrons had deserted him in favor of persons like Désiré Charnay and Louis Aymé, the American consul in Merida, Augustus resolved to find another outlet for publishing his field reports. He saw no reason to continue supplying patrons with the fruits of his research for no compensation, and now, no enthusiasm.

What bothered Augustus was seeing important friends like Salisbury falling under the spell of persons whom Augustus saw more as adventurers than as serious scholars. Charnay, Augustus pointed out, was fast becoming a joke among Mexican scholars, and was being used by certain unethical Mexicans as a source of new and unusual artifacts. Charnay was not a party to any criminal act as far as Augustus knew, but others watching his excavations would loot the sites, later using what information they could extract from him to find artifacts (Augustus Le Plongeon 1880b). In addition, Augustus considered Charnay's photographic record of sites to be superficial and incomplete since he spent only a short time at each site. And there was a dispute over mold making, with Charnay claiming his work was superior to Le Plongeon's. Augustus countered by having experts attest to the exquisite detail of his work.

Aside from the quality and quantity of his work, there was something about Charnay's personality that irritated Augustus. Possibly it was his elitist attitude toward the Maya, or perhaps his official connections with the French government, which had once invaded Mexico. Even though Augustus was also of French parentage, he considered himself an American. Or possibly it was Charnay's accomplishments themselves, which Augustus saw as small considering the financial assistance he received. Not all of Charnay's support came from the French government; the aid from Lorillard and the encouragement from the American Antiquarian Society hit Augustus in a particularly sore spot. Perhaps it was just as well their paths did not cross again after their 1880 encounter in Mexico City.

It was not only a dissatisfaction with the people the society was supporting that distressed Augustus. Increasingly he found himself at odds on issues of scholarship, especially the publishing goals of the society, and with the men who set the policies of the organization. Two of the most influential of these were Joseph Henry and Samuel Haven, who had helped shape the development of the descriptive method in American Archaeology. Their selective editing and publishing of works by other scholars had set in motion the trend away from hypothesizing on incomplete evidence, emphasizing instead the recording of careful observations. They were still in a position to make their opinion of others' work widely known. Such was the case, for instance, in a report to the society in which Haven made unfavorable comments about Le Plongeon. "Like Brasseur," he wrote, "he is an enthusiast, but less guarded and more impetuous" (1877:97).

How could these people argue so strongly for ideas they had concocted while sitting in their offices, Augustus fumed. How could they refuse to accept the true history of the Maya that he and Alice had paid so dearly to uncover? Had he and Alice not given up the pleasures of civilized society for lonely, remote, and uncomfortable habitats? They had tolerated these things willingly, so sure were they that the rewards would more than repay them. Yet to passively sit back and tolerate derision from these supposed peers was more than Augustus could tolerate. There his patience ended.

Le Plongeon's own views, especially on cultural diffusion, continued to differ from the dominant views promoted by Henry, Haven, and others. Since Haven was librarian and manuscript reviewer of the American Antiquarian Society and its *Proceedings* when Augustus was elected a member in 1878, they quickly came into direct conflict. For years Haven had promoted the idea that the American Indian derived from Asia, but "before the existing institutions and national divisions of the parent country were developed" (1856:159). This contradicted Le Plongeon's view that the New World, particularly the Maya, brought civilization to the Old.

An additional source of conflict was a controversy over the interpretations based on the Aztec calendar stone, a monolithic inscribed disk. In 1880 Augustus jumped into a two-year-old battle when he accused Professor Philipp Valentini of having robbed someone else's ideas about the calendar stone and giving a lecture on the subject in New York. Augustus wrote to Salisbury that he had seen letters from Professor Valentini asking Mr. Alfredo Chavero, a Mexican scholar, for the interpretation of several Aztec signs, which he then claimed as his own ideas. According to Augustus, Chavero had already published pamphlets with this information in them in Mexico. Valentini, an important contributor to the *Proceedings* and well thought of in scholarly circles, was furious over the attack on his character and waited for a chance to even the score.

By 1882 it was clear to Augustus that the society would continue publishing what he considered to be works of substandard scholarship by authors who were not well respected by other scholars. This was especially true, he felt, among those who studied the Maya. He could no longer tolerate being linked to these "amateurs" through the society, and in June 1882 Augustus submitted his letter of resignation. He asked for the return of several "objects of antiquity" he had left with the society for safekeeping. His field reports would no longer appear in the *Proceedings*. Instead, he would turn increasingly to other journals such as the *Scientific American* and to his books.

Because some influential members of the Antiquarian Society had been pressuring Salisbury to back the work of the American consul Louis Aymé, Augustus felt compelled to make known his opinions of the man and his qualifications. According to Augustus Aymé was unable to take a decent photo, let alone "even say 'Goodmorning' in the vernacular of Yucatan" (1882a). As far as Augustus was concerned, being unable to communicate with the people whose cultural history was being studied would be an insurmountable handicap.

> I consider it a disgrace to belong to any society of which he is a member; not wishing my name to be dishonored by being associated with his in such connection, or in any other way,

he wrote to Senator George Hoar, then vice president of the society. Not only did Aymé misrepresent himself to scientific societies and use the official diplomatic seal to illegally export Mexican antiquities, said Augustus, but he was also instrumental in an attempt on the Le Plongeons' lives in Uxmal. There was no elaboration of that accusation. Augustus even denounced him for backing out of a duel to protect his own honor after being publicly insulted by a Mexican general. That was no way for any self respecting gentleman to act!

Augustus argued that the society's backing of Aymé would undermine any serious future scientific work in Yucatan.

> I consider it wrong to keep silent longer; knowing that no earnest, true and honest scientific

investigator will come to Yucatan to study the
ancient monuments, and much less stay in the
country on finding himself confronted by such an
individual, armed with certificates of membership
delivered to him by respectable American scientific
societies, backed by an official position granted by
the American government (1882b).

Augustus's position amounted to a demand that the
society choose between Aymé and himself.

As for me, although I have been *nine* years at work,
spent large sums of my own money, made well
known important discoveries . . . and I only
consider my work fairly begun; I will retire from
this field of investigation if [Aymé] remains—and I
will publish to the world my motive for so doing
(1882b).

At least a portion of the feud with Aymé may have stemmed
from Aymé's having sided with Charnay against Augustus in
an earlier dispute.

Augustus's resignation gave Professor Valentini the chance
for revenge that he had been seeking. In a *Proceedings* article
called "The Olmecas and Tultecas," published only three
months later, he included two of Le Plongeon's photographs
from Chichen Itza with captions that suggested they had
been misleadingly retouched. By adding "[supposed]" to "head
of a bearded Itza," Valentini implied that Le Plongeon had
retouched the photos to support his position of Semitic
contact at Chichen Itza.

By then Augustus had turned his back on the American
Antiquarian Society and had returned to Merida with Alice.
Anyone willing to expend the time and money to accompany
them could have seen first hand the bearded figure that
Augustus had photographed.

Chapter 11

A Major Excavation
Recorded

*Though the bones had been completely protected from the air, they
were so rotten that we had to handle them with care for them not to
fall to dust. They seem to have belonged to a small animal with long
and pointed jaws and very pointed teeth. We wrapped each bone in
a separate paper, so that later some qualified person might examine
them.—Alice Le Plongeon in "Dr. Le Plongeon's latest and most
important discoveries among the ruined cities of Yucatan" (Scientific
American 1884a:7146)*

In late 1883 the Le Plongeons returned to Chichen Itza to
excavate what Augustus hoped was the mausoleum of the
High Priest Cay,[1] and record the murals in the Upper Temple
of the Jaguars, or Memorial Hall, overlooking the Ball Court.
They had barely begun their work when they were nearly
driven from the site by a plague of locusts. A mile-wide
column of flying insects passed over Yucatan, descending
on the area and causing great destruction. For seven days
it continued. Live insects devoured crops, and water was
polluted by the millions of dead ones. The people of the
countryside did everything they could to destroy them. They
burned thousands of acres, and hacienda owners paid their
workers by the bushel for dead locusts.

Alice bemoaned the regularity of the plague. "At dusk
they settle, devour what they find, and rest till nine or ten
o'clock the next morning" (1884:7174). Despite all efforts

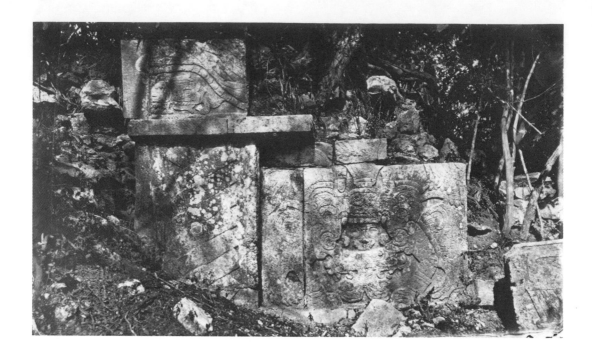

When Augustus found these exposed facing stones from the Platform of Venus at Chichen Itza, he guessed they were a part of another tomb. He took the image of a fish on the upper left block to mean that it was High Priest Cay's tomb, since he had designated the fish as Cay's symbol. 1883. 5 × 8 inch.

to control or destroy them, there was really nothing to do but wait until they left again, following their own mysterious schedule.

Finally, Augustus was able to begin his long-postponed excavation of the Platform of Venus. It had fascinated him since 1875 when his excavation of the nearby Platform of the Eagles uncovered the Chacmool statue. The similarity of shape and size between the two mounds, and their decoration, led him to inspect the Venus platform carefully. On the exposed portion of the structure was the bas-relief of a fish, which Augustus interpreted as the symbol of the High Priest Cay, the brother of warrior Chaacmol. This interpretation was based on the Yucatan Maya word for fish, *cay,* and the assumption that similar structures would be used for similar purposes. Since the 1880 analysis of organic material deposited beside the Chacmool led him to think they were human remains, Augustus assumed he was looking at another burial of an equally important family member. And he expected the platform to contain another statue similar to the Chacmool.

Based on their earlier work, Alice and Augustus had a clear idea of the steps they should take in excavating and recording the mound. They were familiar with the work of their contemporaries, including Heinrich Schliemann, whose excavations of Troy were drawing so much attention and the admonitions of those who would rule out all interpretations from archaeological reports. Alice and Augustus thus

90

recorded their excavation of this mound to clearly show what they actually found, allowing no room for criticism of their interpretation.

Thus they took notes and measurements as they began to clear the Platform of Venus. They drew a plan at a scale of approximately 1 to 100 with the sides measuring 15.9 meters by 15.75 meters. The height was 4 meters. They calculated the position of the structure as north 10 degrees east. Le Plongeon began a 1.5 meter-wide trench in the northwest corner of the platform, away from the stairs, where few facing stones remained. As the workers cut into the mound working toward the center they found rubble core stones with mortar between them.

After eight days of excavating, Le Plongeon's workmen uncovered a sculpture lying on its back about 1.5 meters north of the center of the platform at ground level. Alice recorded the excavation and reported its results in *Scientific American*. "The figure was thickly coated with loose mortar. One leg was broken off below the knee, but we found it under the figure, and afterward adjusted it in place to make a picture" (1884a:7145).

Alice described the sculpture in detail, giving its dimensions and colors, and noting that the shell fingernails and toenails had become separated from the figure. The statue rested on small "conodial pillars" laid on their sides as part of a configuration of 182 cones covering about eight square meters. "Two-thirds of the pillars are painted blue and one-third red; they vary in height from eighty centimeters to one meter twenty-five centimeters."

Augustus drew a cross section of the platform, showing the cones piled in neat rows up to four deep, with some clusters oriented north-south and others east-west. Some were on, and others were below the ground-level floor, which Augustus indicated by a double line four meters below the top of the platform.[2]

"On a level with the pillars were twelve serpent heads," oriented in various directions. Alice described their decorations and colors which had survived undisturbed within the structure. "From the top of each head rises a kind of plume or perhaps flame, and on each side of the front of the head perpendicular ornaments like horns." The heads were painted green and had feathers incised on the upper part. Their undersides were covered with serpent scales. The edges of the jaws were also yellow, while the forked tongue and the gums were red. The teeth were white. Around the eyes and "over the brow" was blue and the eyes were filled with a white "shell." The horns or nose plugs projecting from

Above: As the Le Plongeons directed excavations into the Platform of Venus, they carefully recorded what they found. This written version of a cross section includes measurements, descriptions, and a sketch coded by numbers to the items found. "Sacred monkey laying on its back," "1. Twelve snake heads," "5. A fine red floor—5.60 m below summit and 1.10 m below white floor," "7. Mother Earth and disappointment." Opposite page: On a page from the Platform of Venus field notes, the Le Plongeons recorded the dimensions and direction of the mound. They included six different measurements of the steps. Written at Chichen Itza in 1883.

Direction of mound

North ten degrees ~~north~~ East

Width of staircase   3ᵐ 90°

Height of each step   0ᵐ, 30°

width of each step   0ᵐ, 28°

Length or depth of staircase   4ᵐ, 00

From staircase to corner   7ᵐ, 50

Top of mound from corner to stairs   6ᵐ, 00

Width of top from E. to West.   16ᵐ, 00°

Do — — N. & South   16ᵐ, 00

Depth of first statue from top   4, 00

9 - 80

13 steps

1ᵐ 50

7ᵐ 50

365

1½ 3 2½

19/15

550
550
550
6

the snout were green, and tipped in red as was the "feather" on the top. Alice lamented the broken condition of the heads and suggested that they had been fractured at the time of their interment.

Within the concentration of stone cones, the excavators also found a stone urn set into the floor. Inside it were a flat "trapezoidal . . . green jade with a human face—full face," two half beads of jadeite, a jade tube, a spherical crystal described as "a ball of white glass nearly an inch in diameter, and the remains of a mosaic."

The excavation continued through three earlier floor levels which Augustus plotted in his cross section and described in the field notes. The upper two were painted red and the lower was yellow. On the floors they encountered more artifacts, including an obsidian projectile point, shards of "fine pottery," and the bones of a small animal. The final floor, at bedrock, was painted red.[3]

After they reached the lowest level, Augustus next directed his Maya workers to dig a trench to the southwest. There they uncovered a number of flat stones carved in low relief. The red floor extended farther south. Lying on it, face down, was "another stone with a fish sculptured on it, the fish being surrounded by the fold of a serpent's body." The Le Plongeons were convinced that they were excavating the burial chamber of the high priest Cay, noting all their observations in the excavation notes and drawings.

The record they created, along with photographs of the operation, was on a par with the work of their contemporaries, both self-taught and formally trained. And as yet there was no one else working in Yucatan to confer with or compare results. If they could have been satisfied with only recording observations and gathering data, as influential academicians such as Henry and Haven were demanding, they probably would have continued to be noted as fine researchers. But the more information they gathered, the more they speculated. The pieces to the puzzle of Maya history Augustus had created fell in place too easily for their own good. The Platform of Venus excavation and the discovery of the Chacmool not only made them more committed to their ill-conceived ideas on Maya history, but also hastened their ostracism from scientific circles.

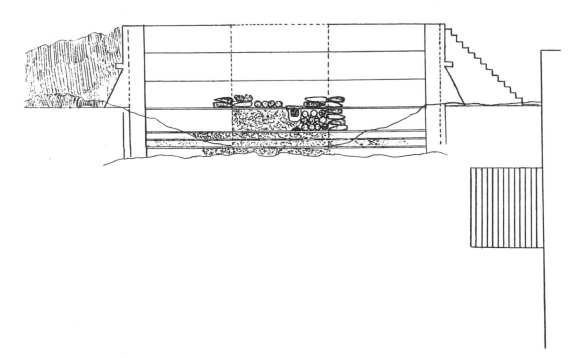

Above: Le Plongeon drew a cross section of the Platform of Venus showing the position of conical-shaped stones and an urn as uncovered during the excavation. The darker shaded cones were blue; the others, orange. The double lines indicate floors uncovered—the bottom two are red. This cross section is the first by any archaeologist working in the Maya area. Drawn circa 1883. Courtesy of the Latin American Library, Tulane University. Below: Le Plongeon's restoration drawing of the Platform of Venus included a detailed record of the existing decorative panels along with speculation based on their excavations. The drawing was photographed by Le Plongeon who added the foreground and cloudy sky from other photographs, creating a composite print. The date of the photograph is not known, but it was published in Augustus Le Plongeon's "The Origins of the Egyptians" in 1913.

95

Above: Facing stone uncovered during excavation of the Platform of Venus. Finely carved lines were preserved because stone was covered. A comparison of this 1883 photo with the actual stone today shows that a century of exposure has greatly eroded the relief. 5 × 8 inch. Below: The current condition of the facing stone from the Platform of Venus, first uncovered and photographed in 1883 by Le Plongeon. Extensive weathering can be seen in this photo made in 1980. Photograph by Lawrence G. Desmond.

*Above: Le Plongeon effectively used both drawings and photos to
record objects found in the excavation of the Platform of Venus. In
this photo, tenoned serpent heads, conical-shaped stones, and a large
stone urn are shown in situ. 1883. 5 × 8 inch. Below: As workers
removed the stone cones from the deep trench in the Platform of
Venus, they no doubt noticed the tonal quality of the stones. 1883.
5 × 8 inch glass plate negative is cracked.*

A noticeably aged Augustus Le Plongeon poses with serpent sculptures and urn removed from the Platform of Venus at Chichen Itza. Many details of the serpents described in Alice's account of the excavation, including colors and elements protruding from the head, have now been lost. 1883. 5 × 8 inch.

Though it was not their intention, this period at Chichen Itza was to be the last fieldwork in Yucatan for Alice and Augustus. Perhaps sensing this, they continued their recording with a sense of urgency. As they prepared to leave Chichen Itza, the Le Plongeons made notes on other bas-reliefs around the site. At the north of the huge Ball Court stood a small temple with many reliefs. Round stone columns supporting the front of its roof arch were covered with warriors and other designs. Alice described the temple for *Scientific American:*

> The back wall and sides of this box are covered
> with bas-reliefs that do great credit to the dead and
> forgotten artists. They represent human figures in
> various dresses and attitudes and landscapes. There
> is one face with Semitic features and full beard
> (1884a:7147).[4]

They returned to the murals in the Upper Temple of the Jaguars to finish tracing them. To their dismay they found the murals damaged beyond repair with whole segments too defaced to interpret. Apparently the damage was caused by the carelessness of a recent visitor, Louis Aymé.

Alice made little attempt to hide the identity of the perpetrator when her account of the discovery was published.

> To our grief, we at once saw that some one had
> tried to clean the wall by *scratching* off the dirt. In

answer to our exclamations of disgust, some of the soldiers that escorted us in our expedition said "Oh, yes! that gentleman who came two years ago did it; he scraped it with a machete, and said 'Look at this ugly old woman.' "

Alice's first thought was that Désiré Charnay had done it. "No," said the soldier, "it was M. ———, the Consul Americano, who accompanied M. Charnay."

Alice and Augustus were soon to feel the repercussions of this bold revelation. Aymé was a close friend of Stephen Salisbury, Jr., who had important political connections throughout the eastern United States, and the loss of his friendship, though it was temporary, was a severe blow to the Le Plongeons.

While still in Yucatan Augustus may not have realized the extent of the damage he was bringing to his own career as a Maya archaeologist by making examples of people like Aymé, as well as attacking Aymé in his letter of resignation. Instead while on-site and seeing directly the destruction that was occurring there, he and Alice felt obligated to expose, and, they hoped, stop the guilty parties. After all Yucatan was their life; the Maya, their family.

Chapter 12

Queen Móo's Story

Móo, we learn from her pictures, was a very pretty girl, but she was the cause of great political and religious disturbances. Aac loved her, so did Chaacmol. To marry one of her brothers was legal; but she could not marry two of them. She chose the warrior Chaacmol.—Alice Le Plongeon in "Ruined Uxmal" (The New York World, *June 27, 1881a*)

It felt good to be back in Brooklyn, for a while at least. There were stacks of fieldnotes and drawings to go over. *Scientific American* was interested in publishing more articles on the Maya, and Alice readily found outlets for her articles on life in Yucatan. Both she and Augustus continued to work on books about the places and people they knew so well. But they hoped for other projects that would allow them to confront the American audience with the wonders of Maya civilization.

One such opportunity seemed to be developing shortly after their return to Brooklyn. Augustus learned that there might be a possibility of creating a small Maya temple from his molds at the New Orleans Exposition. Mr. Burke, director of the exposition, invited the Le Plongeons to come to New Orleans and work on the building. There was one catch, however. Burke needed five thousand dollars to construct the building with fireproof materials; otherwise the exhibition could not be covered by fire insurance. President Díaz offered space already allocated to the Mexican government for its part in the exposition but could give no financial assistance.

Spencer Baird at the Smithsonian was contacted to see if that organization could assist, but the Smithsonian did not consider the project important enough to spend five thousand dollars—a considerable amount of money in 1884. With reluctance, Augustus dropped the project. Instead he and Alice turned their full attention to manuscript writing.

Augustus concentrated on re-creating the ancient history of the Maya and their supposed link to other cultures. Using murals, sculptures, and bas-reliefs from Uxmal and Chichen Itza, Augustus narrated a life history of several key Maya rulers. He used material remains from their excavations to support his interpretation which appeared full-blown in *Sacred Mysteries Among the Mayas and Quiches, 11,500 Years Ago.* The book synthesized Augustus's findings in Yucatan, or "Mayax," as he called the land of the Maya. It set forth his theories on Maya connections with Freemasonry and the civilizations of the Middle East. It narrated the story he and Alice felt was graphically illustrated on the walls of the Upper Temple of the Jaguars.

Sacred Mysteries told of the love between Queen Móo and Prince Coh, of Prince Coh's death at the hands of his brother Aac, and of Queen Móo's final escape to Egypt where she was welcomed as *Isis* (translated by Le Plongeon to mean little sister). The story told in the murals was substantiated, Augustus felt, by the excavation of what he interpreted as the cremated remains of Prince Coh.

> Nowhere, except in Mayax, do we find it [the physical evidence] as forming part of the history of the nation. Nowhere, except in Mayax, do we find the portrait of the actors in the tragedy. There, we not only see their portraits carried in bas-relief, on stone or wood, or their marble statues in the round, or represented in the mural paintings that adorn the walls of the funeral chamber built to the memory of the victim, but we discover the ornaments they wore, the weapons they used, nay, more, their mortal remains (1886:84).

He wove his own analysis and explanation into the telling of the history. "It was among the Mayas," he wrote, "that the youngest of brothers should marry the eldest of sisters, to insure the legitimate and divine descent of the royal family." He did not divulge whether this information came from some ethnographic or archaeological evidence he had but felt it was useful in understanding the family of Queen Móo.

The story opened during the "ancient epoch," portraying the royal family in residence at Uxmal: the sovereign, Canchi; his wife, Zoc; eldest son, Prince Cay (later to become high priest); Prince Aac; the youngest son, Prince Coh; Princess Móo; and Princess Nicté.

Augustus described how Princess Móo became queen of Chichen Itza after the death of her father and how she married the great warrior Prince Coh, whom she loved. Uxmal had been inherited by Prince Aac, but he coveted Queen Móo and was jealous of the fame of Coh. He conspired to kill his brother Coh, capture and marry Queen Móo, and unite the divided empire under himself. He murdered Coh, and civil war broke out, which Aac offered to stop if Queen Móo would accept his romantic advances. She rejected him, and his armies finally defeated her followers. Sometime after her capture she escaped with the help of friends, but her brother Cay was put to death.

Augustus wrote of Aac,

> In token of his victory, Aac caused his statue—the
> feet resting on the flayed bodies of his kind, their
> heads being suspended from his belt—to be placed
> over the main entrance of the royal palace at
> Uxmal, where, as I have said, its remains may be
> seen today.

Augustus attributed other construction at Uxmal to Prince Aac, including the north and south wings of the Governor's Palace where the sculpture they thought was Móo's portrait was found, and the House of the Turtles, built as Aac's private residence.

He finished this version of Maya history with Queen Móo's death:

> After her death she received the honors of
> apotheosis; became the goddess of fire, and was
> worshipped in a magnificent temple, built on the
> summit of a high and very extensive pyramid whose
> ruins are still to be seen in the city of Izamal.

⌐⌐ ⌐⌐ ⌐⌐

Augustus and Alice continued to write and lecture extensively. In 1886 Alice published *Here and There in Yucatan*, a collection of previously published accounts of some of their journeys in Yucatan, including their 1876–77 boat trip from Progreso to Belize. The *New York Times* praised her style, calling it "direct and simple." Alice read a paper before the New York Academy of Sciences in 1886, titled "Yucatan, its Ancient Temples and Palaces," and another in 1887, "Eastern Yucatan, its Scenery, People, and Ancient Cities and Monuments." She also published an article that year, "The Mayas: Their customs, laws and religions" in the *Magazine of American History*. Augustus worked on a lengthy manuscript which he called "Monuments of Mayax and their Historical Teachings." It was never published.

The Le Plongeons also wrote to the American Association for the Advancement of Science, requesting permission to present papers at their August 10–17, 1887 meeting. Alice proposed to give a slide lecture on the archaeology of Yucatan. Augustus had written a paper called "Ancient American Civilization." They waited expectantly for notice of acceptance, not anticipating any problems. After all, Daniel Brinton, vice-president of the anthropological section of the association, and the official who would issue the invitations to speak, had written favorably of them in a November 1885 letter published in the *American Antiquarian*. Referring to a pleasant evening spent with the Le Plongeons, he had praised the efforts of Augustus and "his accomplished wife" to correct the "hasty conclusions of Charnay," adding the caveat, "despite whatever opinion one may entertain of the analogies the doctor thinks he has discovered between the Maya culture and language and those of Asia and Africa" (1885:378).

Brinton's replies to the Le Plongeons' request to speak at the meetings were not only cool, but suspiciously late. Brinton's letter to Alice, dated August 13, three days after the association meetings began, said that while the members all agreed such a lecture would be of great value, all the evening lecture rooms were occupied, and the only space available was a room during the day that could not be darkened. Further, they could only allow Alice thirty minutes to cover her topic.

Apparently embarrassed by his late reply, Brinton added that he had written his response on August 5 and had entrusted it to an assistant who "placed an erroneous address upon it." However, he failed to explain why a letter written on August 5 was dated August 13. Brinton's reply to Augustus was not received until three weeks after the close of the meeting, having been sent via San Francisco.

Though disappointed by this apparent rebuff, Alice and Augustus carried on with their writing and speaking about Yucatan. They were negotiating with museums and individuals to buy some of the molds from Uxmal and Chichen Itza to raise much-needed cash. Though the molds were

Daniel G. Brinton, 1837–1899. Professor of American Linguistics and Archaeology at the University of Pennsylvania. He opposed much of Le Plongeon's work, and accused him of being "eccentric." Courtesy of the American Philosophical Society.

unique and of excellent quality, the search for buyers dragged on for years. The Le Plongeons did have some financial support from a few individuals who thought their work was important. And there were some royalties from the sale of *Sacred Mysteries*.

Others who realized the value of their work were less interested in the well-being of the Le Plongeons, instead making unauthorized use of their materials. It was impossible to determine if certain instances were intentional deceptions or merely misunderstandings. In January 1889, for instance, they were invited to attend a lecture in New York by the traveler Frederick Ober, who had written *Travels in Mexico*. To their great shock, they saw their own photos projected on the screen during Ober's talk.

> Imagine our amazement when he threw upon the
> screen wretched copies of the east facade of the
> Palace at Chichen—made from imperfect prints that
> he had begged from Mrs. Le Plongeon for his
> album, and she having given him with the
> understanding that he should not use them either in
> his lectures or articles.

While Ober coolly took credit for the photos, Augustus guessed that he had never even visited Chichen Itza. Noting that Alice appeared among the workmen in the foreground of the pictures, Augustus added, "We expected that he would complete the story by pointing at Mrs. Le Plongeon's picture and say—Here is my wife:—he did not, happily" (1889).

105

Alice Dixon Le Plongeon, circa 1890, in New York. By now Alice and Augustus had left fieldwork behind and were publishing articles and books based on their interpretations. 5 × 8 inch.

Their only defense against such encroachments was to continue publishing their own research as quickly as possible. Augustus worked on a long manuscript revising and elaborating the history of the Maya. He hoped it would sell at least as well as *Sacred Mysteries.* Alice concentrated on the shorter articles that journals and magazines were anxious to carry.

One article, "The Mayas," appeared in an 1890 volume of *Theosophical Siftings,* published by the Theosophical Publishing Society of London. Alice may have been a student of the theosophical movement, which was experiencing a wave of popularity at the time. Its emphasis on spiritual insights and revelations would have struck a harmonious cord in Alice, whose writings about Yucatan were beginning to emphasize metaphysical matters. If there was a connection, it may have been through Madame Helena P. Blavatsky in New York, a leader in the movement. She had spent time with spiritual masters in India and brought knowledge learned from them to her followers in England and America. Her multi-volume treatise, *The Secret Doctrine,* published in 1888, made several references to Augustus's work in a discussion of Central America.

⌐⌐ ⌐⌐ ⌐⌐

In 1890 Augustus gave seven lectures to the Lowell Institute on "Ancient American Civilization." These lectures were illustrated with slides covering the ethnology of Yucatan, the history of the conquest, Maya language, development of architecture, and a detailed look at Chichen Itza's architecture and history, based on his interpretations of the murals in the Upper Temple of the Jaguars.

That same year a book by Daniel Brinton, now professor of American Archaeology at the University of Pennsylvania, appeared, fanning the smoldering animosity between him and Augustus into an open feud. In the book, *Essays of an Americanist,* he charged Augustus with "eccentricity" for asserting that the basic unit of measure among the Maya was the meter. This implied that Augustus believed the Maya knew the distance between the equator and the pole, which was the basis of calculations for the meter.

Brinton contended that the Maya used the cubit, a measurement based on human anatomy, specifically the distance from the elbow to the finger tip. It was just one of several charges, all calculated to discredit Augustus, but he would not let Brinton get away with the affront.

Chapter 13

Surviving on the Fringe

On seeing his book printed, my scholarly husband would feel that his life work had not been lost. At present he is very unhappy about it, having met with no financial assistance in his great task. Each one of the many whom I have approached on the matter has left it for someone else to do, advising me to see other persons till my soul is sick with disappointments!—Letter from Alice Le Plongeon to Phoebe A. Hearst (probably 1896)

It was a pleasant change of pace for the Le Plongeons to travel to Europe in 1891. Alice had a reunion with her brothers and sisters in London after eighteen years in America. For her it was like being a tourist. They visited the Crystal Palace, Westminster Abbey, and Covent Garden, and they heard a musical program performed by the band of the Royal Horse Guards. She and her husband, with his flowing white beard and brooding wild eyes, were treated as explorers and adventurers from unknown lands. Their stories and observations were fresh and exotic, and Alice's family and friends were a delighted and uncriticizing audience. The round of parties and visits were but a pleasant respite, however. After two months, the Le Plongeons returned to New York, where their financial and scholarly battles continued.

Augustus could not let Daniel Brinton's public attack of the previous year go unanswered. He challenged Brinton to a scholarly debate on the many details of Maya studies that Brinton discussed in *Essays of an Americanist,* including Maya prophecies, science and numbers, and cosmogeny. The challenge appeared in the *New York Advertiser* in 1893. There was no response.

In 1894 Augustus repeated the challenge in the *Brooklyn Eagle,* accusing Brinton of posing as *the* authority on the Maya in the United States and impeding the progress of American archaeology.

> Hoping, sir, that you will gladly improve the opportunity to show that you are really superior an authority, with right therefore to criticize others on such an important subject, to all American scientists, and afford me one for displaying my extravagancies or eccentricities before the members of the American Association for the Advancement of Science, I beg to subscribe myself (1896:206).

The debate was never held. Le Plongeon included his challenge in an appendix to *Queen Móo and the Egyptian Sphinx,* adding this lament, "Dr. Brinton took no more notice of this challenge than he had taken of the former one."

Considered an excellent scholar and strategist, Brinton wisely chose not to engage in an open debate before his peers with a man who had studied the ancient Maya, not only through archival sources, but by living with their descendants in and about the ruins. Augustus also spoke Yucatec Maya, having learned it from his Maya excavators, and from his friend, Father Crescencio Carrillo y Ancona of Merida.

Augustus felt that deciphering the ancient Maya script required a knowledge of spoken Maya, a point which Brinton had already conceded to him in a letter. He knew full well that Brinton had never been in the field, and thus had a limited knowledge of many of the fine points of Maya ethnology and archaeology, other than those gleaned from field researchers such as Dr. Karl Berendt, a linguist who was working in Central America, and who maintained close contact with Brinton. And for Brinton to agree to a public debate was tantamount to admitting that Le Plongeon was on his own intellectual level and had serious things to say.

Le Plongeon found that the more intensely he defended his position, the more the opposition found in it to attack. He still had many friends in Mexico, however. Bishop Carrillo y Ancona referred to him as "our good friend Le Plongeon" in the *Anales del Museo Nacional,* the official publication of the National Museum in Mexico City. But they were of little help to him in dealing with the American scholars. He could not even find a publisher for *Queen Móo and the Egyptian Sphinx,* his major work in which he would divulge clues "to the American hieroglyphs" and decipher some of them.

Since personal funds for publishing were lacking, Alice stepped in on behalf of her husband and wrote Phoebe A. Hearst, wife of the publishing magnate William Randolph Hearst, asking for assistance. She argued that the book would "give to America its true place among the nations of antiquity." In response Mrs. Hearst provided funds to cover part of the costs.

In the preface of *Queen Móo* Augustus alluded to the difficulties his unpopular theories were causing.

> I have been accused of promulgating notions on ancient America contrary to the opinion of men regarded as authorities on American Archaeology. And so it is, indeed. Mine is not the fault, however, although it may be my misfortune, since it has surely entailed upon me their enmity and its consequences.

Daniel Brinton and his colleagues in the American Association for the Advancement of Science were on his mind as he continued,

> But who are those pretended authorities? Certainly not the doctors and professors at the head of the universities and colleges in the U.S.; for not only do they know absolutely nothing of Ancient American civilization, but, judging from letters in my possession, the majority of them refuse to learn anything concerning it.

Queen Móo and the Egyptian Sphinx was to stand as his last major published work on the Maya until after his death. It was an expanded version of the Queen Móo story introduced a decade earlier in *Sacred Mysteries. Queen Móo* was reviewed in the London *Athenaeum.* This second book on Queen Móo and Maya civilization was called "well-printed and well-illustrated." But the reviewer found the text to be disappointing, full of "statements in all seriousness, which show that the author is more often led by his imagination than by his knowledge."

Queen Móo included drawings from the Upper Temple of the Jaguars to illustrate Queen Móo's life story, including her travels to Egypt. To reinforce this slice of Maya history Augustus added evidence he found during his 1875 and 1883 excavations at Chichen Itza. In his interpretation, Queen Móo ordered the Upper Temple of the Jaguars to be erected in Prince Coh's honor. She also called for construction of the Platform of the Eagles and Jaguars as a mausoleum to contain the cremated remains of his body. A similar mausoleum, the Platform of Venus, was built nearby in honor of High Priest Cay.

He interpreted the iconography on the Upper Temple of the Jaguars to read "Cay, the high priest, desires to bear witness that Móo has made this offering, earnestly invoking Coh, the warrior of warriors."

After the construction of the two burial monuments at Chichen Itza, Augustus wrote, Queen Móo fled to the Antilles, which he called Zinaan. Not feeling safe there, Queen Móo resolved to travel on to one of the remaining islands of sunken Atlantis. But she found no islands, so she continued her journey to Egypt where she was given a warm welcome. Augustus bolstered this version with a new interpretation of the lintel in the Akab Dzib, stating that it told of the destruction of Atlantis. As in his first interpretation of the lintel, Augustus offered neither a glyph-by-glyph translation, nor an explanation of his methodology.

While Augustus focused on the development of Queen Móo's story, Alice continued her efforts to resolve the issue of the molds held by the American Museum of Natural History. In 1894 Marshall H. Saville, assistant curator of ethnology at the museum, attempted to raise enough money to acquire the Le Plongeon molds and tracings of the frescos from the Upper Temple of the Jaguars at Chichen Itza.

Later Alice described the affair in a letter to Phoebe Hearst. The molds and some casts were "received in the museum," but "no subscription was started, nor were the casts exhibited." Museum officials asked Alice to give a private lecture to Mrs. Jesup, wife of the president of the museum and her coterie. Alice was assured that her presence would guarantee a successful fund-raising effort.

> As I was the only woman who had explored the
> Yucatan Ruins and accomplished something in
> American archaeology, Mrs. Jesup would, among
> her lady friends, make a subscription to donate the
> collection to the museum (1900a).

The lecture went very well. Professor Putnam, an important archaeologist at the Peabody Museum, "rose and stated that my lecture was the best exposition of the subject he had ever listened to." But, to Alice's dismay, no one made a move to contribute toward the acquisition of the molds. Instead,

The only result of the lecture was a severe illness to me. This was induced by extreme depression through disappointment at seeing no action taken at the close of the meeting, and also by a severe chill, because we walked under a drenching rain without umbrella from the Museum to the elevated railway, and I was at the time only convalescing from grippe."

Mr. Loubat, a patron of the arts, then made a suspiciously miserly offer for the purchase of the molds. When the Le Plongeons refused it, he had other casts made in Paris, which, according to Alice, were of inferior quality. She and Augustus strongly suspected that Mr. Loubat's offer to purchase their molds for almost nothing and his subsequent action in having more expensive ones made in Paris was "done with unkind purpose." He donated them to the museum, which effectively blocked the acquisition of similar objects, including the Le Plongeons' molds, "no matter how superior these might be."

This failure to obtain funding was a serious blow to the continuation of their work, Alice explained to Mrs. Hearst. "As we spent *all* our means in those explorations, expecting to replenish our purse by the sale of our work, our researches came to a standstill."

There was irony in this financial crisis that stopped their fieldwork. Alice's work was appearing regularly in well-known periodicals including the *Magazine of American History* and *Popular Science*. And in 1895 *Scientific American* had recognized her as one of a score of women "who have contributed vastly to the knowledge and culture of the age." It appears that, indeed, it was the publication of Augustus's lifework, the story of Queen Móo, that dealt the final blow to his credibility in the mainstream scholarly community and made it impossible for him to raise funds.

◻ ◻ ◻

In 1897 Augustus and Alice visited London again. On the ship returning to New York, they met Elbert Hubbard, who was reviewing *Queen Móo* for a journal called *The Arena*. Hubbard was impressed by the sprightliness of the old doctor, who was then over seventy years old.

Dr. Le Plongeon may be sixty, seventy, or ninety years of age. He is becoming bald, has a long snowy, patriarchal beard, bright blue eyes, and a beautiful brick dust complexion. When every

passenger on board had lost appetite and animation,
this sturdy old man trod the upper deck and
laughed at the storm as the winds sang through the
cordage of the trembling ship (1897:343).

Hubbard was also quite taken with Alice, "his faithful coadjutor, collaborator, and companion." When she gave a little lecture to the other passengers, "it was voted a great treat." Hubbard concluded that "Madam Le Plongeon is a rare woman; . . . My private opinion is that she is of a little better fibre than her husband, in which remark I am quite sure I should be backed by the learned doctor himself."

As for his opinion of *Queen Móo and the Egyptian Sphinx,* Mr. Hubbard wrote, "The work is intensely interesting, even to a layman, and in its bold statements is sure to awaken into life a deal of dozing thought, and some right lively opposition as well."

While under fire for his historical interpretations of the Maya, Augustus was still considered an expert on the Maya language. In the fall of 1902, William J. McGee of the Smithsonian Institution requested comments from him concerning three Maya dictionaries that the Smithsonian proposed to publish. Augustus provided McGee with a thorough background on the origin of each dictionary, as well as a review of the linguistic merits of each.

One of them, named after a town in Yucatan where the information was supposedly collected, had been in the possession of Daniel Brinton. The Motul Dictionary owned by Brinton was not worth publishing, Le Plongeon explained, since it was an unedited mix of linguistic material compiled partly from the Ciudad Real Dictionary in the Brown University Library, and partly from modern linguistic informants who assisted Karl Berendt. One of Brinton's chief sources of raw field data, Berendt had died of an overdose of morphine in the village of Coban, Guatemala. According to Le Plongeon, after Berendt's untimely death, someone seized his papers and sold them to a bookseller in New York, who in turn sold them to Dr. Brinton.

With regard to Brinton's scholarly merits, Le Plongeon continued in his letter to Mr. McGee,

> I accuse Dr. Brinton of impeding the progress of
> Maya ethnology in this country by publishing books
> on a subject of which he knew *absolutely* nothing,
> and of using the notes of Dr. Berendt and palming
> them on his reader as his own knowledge.

In his zeal to debunk the impression that Brinton had any linguistic expertise, Le Plongeon ignored Brinton's comment about the Motul Dictionary in *Essays of an Americanist*. "Only two copies of it are in existence, one, very carefully made, with numerous notes, by Dr. Berendt, is in my possession" (1890:119).

Le Plongeon simply could not tolerate supposedly scholarly efforts to interpret the Maya by those who lacked the basic skill of knowing their language. Since he had lived in their midst and could speak directly to them, he believed his interpretations of Maya history to be true. For Augustus, his translations of murals and hieroglyphic inscriptions and his analysis of excavations based on the history he created were the most accurate scholarship available at the time.

His confidence in his own linguistic facility led Augustus to one of the most controversial speculations in his writings. In trying to neatly tie up the loose ends of his diffusionist theories, he offered further proof that the Maya brought civilization to Egypt thousands of years ago, by arguing that Christ's last words on the cross were spoken in Maya. Finding a loose phonetic connection between Aramaic and Maya, Augustus stated that the recording of those words in the New Testament (Matt. 27:46) was incorrect. Instead of Aramaic, "Eli, Eli, lamah sabachthani," he suggested it should be read as Yucatec Maya, "Hele, Hele, lamah zabac ta ni," or "Now, now, I am fainting, darkness covers my face" (1896:38). Part of his argument rested on his position that the last words of Christ in Aramaic, that God had forsaken him, were inappropriate to a personage such as Christ.

Augustus's stubbornness in trying to defend unfounded statements such as this served to seal his fate among the rapidly growing circle of intellectuals who were acquiring status and university backing. While these were busy positioning themselves in the development of an institutionalized discipline, Augustus and Alice had been immersed in a rigorous field experience that led them to propose untested hypotheses. Increasingly they found themselves excluded from the very circle they wanted to join.

Chapter 14

Immortalizing
the Epic

*From the standpoint of purely human interest, what undoubtedly
will make the greatest appeal is the Le Plongeons' tracings, by close
examination of every object found, the story of the fall of the once
mighty Maya empire, concluding with the flight of her last Queen to
Egypt. This story has its counterpart in the myth of Isis and Osiris,
and Dr. Le Plongeon read also a parallel account in the celebrated
Troano MS.—Undated review of* The Fall of Maya *by Brooks Betts,
1911*

By March of 1900 Augustus's health had broken. He and
Alice had all but given up hope of raising money to
return to Yucatan. She spoke candidly to Phoebe Hearst,
their benefactor, in a letter dated March 17.

> Since 1885 we have tried our best to dispose of our
> moulds, but have met with opposition and
> disappointment on all sides, because our studies did
> not tally with old ideas of certain professors; and
> meanwhile we have lectured in order to live, and to
> make known ancient American civilization while
> writing the results of our researches.

They had lived on the royalties from the 1886 publication of *Sacred Mysteries* until the book was sold out. "While
the book was in the market we managed, with very strict
economy, to live from its proceeds, at the same time writing
other volumes."

She begged Mrs. Hearst, who planned to fund a major search for American relics for the archaeological museum at Berkeley, to consider their materials.

> We have ready for use more than could possibly be acquired in that quarter at the present time, and we also possess the knowledge to make plain the meaning of these interesting sculptures.

In another letter the following day, Alice gave details of her husband's painful heart ailment, angina pectoris. "He is unable to take solid food, and should have an immediate change of climate. He is the victim of conservative opponents, and his condition is undoubtedly the result of prolonged disappointment and anxiety." Yet he continued writing, hoping to publish one more monumental work.

Spurred perhaps by love for her dying husband, and inspired certainly by his grand history of the Maya, Alice wrote an epic poem about Queen Móo and Prince Coh. In 1902 *Queen Móo's Talisman* was published in New York. The dedication in *Talisman* reflected Alice's gratitude for the support Augustus always gave her career. "To Doctor Le Plongeon, whose works inspired these pages, their author dedicates them; not as a worthy offering, but as a small token of loving endeavor to gratify his oft expressed desire."

Queen Móo's Talisman represented a radical shift in Alice's literary career. Unlike her previous journalistic and historical pieces about Yucatan, or the detailed description of excavations, this was a piece of fiction set in verse, and based on Augustus's theories and their historical analysis of the Maya. The two of them appear as central figures, drawn by "relentless forces" to study the Maya.

> To learn the past, Maya-land both turned,
> But no faint ray of mem'ry in them burned
> Altho' he murmured in a certain place—
> "Familiar 'tis, there's something I would trace."

The spiritual connection the Le Plongeons felt during their work at Chichen Itza, reflected in the title of the poem, was symbolized by the cylindrical jade piece found in what they had called Prince Coh's Tomb.

> Within a white stone urn in ancient tomb.
> Charred heart and talisman lay in the gloom.
> To her he gave the gem.—"Now take thine own,
> I pray: henceforth it must be thine alone."

If Alice and Augustus ever believed themselves to be Queen Móo and Prince Coh reincarnated, then *Queen Móo's Talisman* was their confession of it and a documentation of their ancient memories. If not it was a clever literary vehicle, keeping the reader involved. The immortal spirit of Prince Aac returned to converse with Alice, hoping to come back to life through her.

> To her he turned again:—Forgive! forgive!
> Earth-born thro' thee. ah! let me once more live.
> My crimes and victories, *my soul's defeat,*
> My anguish and remorse, wilt thou repeat;
> For thus alone new life may dawn for me—
> In solitude I've long awaited me.

The metaphysical overtones and emphasis on immortality may have served to bolster the Le Plongeons in a time of deteriorating health and a worsening financial situation. In 1902, the same year that *Talisman* was published, Alice wrote a letter to Frederick W. Putnam at the American Museum of Natural History, offering for sale seven small pieces they had found twenty years earlier in Yucatan. Of great sentimental value, the collection included two sections of wooden beam, a piece she described as a crude bear's head, a flint point, a stone attached to a handle, and two pieces of stone sculpture from the center section of the east facade of the Governor's Palace at Uxmal. These they identified as the head of High Priest Cay and the torso of Prince Coh.

Putnam knew the Le Plongeons well and sympathized with their plight. He wrote a memo to Jesup, the museum president, recommending strongly that the seven pieces be acquired. "I know how hard it is for them to offer to dispose of these objects which they brought from Yucatan many years ago." They were purchased for a small sum and eventually a few were placed on display.

In 1904 a book reviewer for the *American Antiquarian and Oriental Journal*, C. S. Wake, reviewed Dr. Le Plongeon's *Queen Móo and the Egyptian Sphinx*. Wake tried to be even-handed. His tone was measured and conservative; his review was an analysis of Augustus's theories, pointing out the limitations of the opposing theories. Wake praised the Le Plongeons' fieldwork, asking "Why, then, have they [scholars] practically agreed to taboo the work he has done?" Perhaps the time was not right to accept his new ideas, although after eighteen years, "we ought to see signs of its approach," suggested Wake.

"Specialists are very apt to look with an unfavorable eye on anything outside of their own particular specialty, particularly . . . the work of an 'amateur,' or, let us say, a non-professional," continued Wake, referring to Le Plongeon's position outside the professional circle of scholars.

Wake concluded that no one had taken up Augustus's challenge to translate a particular legend on a frieze, not because they lacked linguistic skills, but "because there is something radically wrong in the author's explanation of the facts."

The facts he referred to were the relative antiquity of America versus Egypt and Babylonia, and the transoceanic contact between them. Wake agreed with Le Plongeon, to a degree, that "there was communication between the two continents for a long period," but he pointed out that Egypt and Babylonia were important civilizations far earlier than Mesoamerica. "None the less," Wake wrote, "Dr. Le Plongeon is to be congratulated on the good work he has done in collecting information which will aid largely someday in deciding the important question of American origins."

Any published acknowledgment of Le Plongeon's work, even a lukewarm review, was a welcome occurrence since many chose to ignore it. Alice Le Plongeon was earning some public appreciation and acclaim in literary circles for *Queen Móo's Talisman,* which led her and Augustus to think about transforming it into a drama. After a careful search for a sympathetic author, they gave exclusive right of dramatization to Brooks Betts. His brother M. Beverly was to write a musical accompaniment based on Maya chants and dances. Alice supervised the writing of the drama, *The fall of Maya,* which was completed shortly before she died.

On March 4, 1905 Alice wrote her last letter to Phoebe Hearst.

> I am sorry to report that Dr. Le Plongeon since his severe illness has been less well than before that event, and this winter has tried him severely. Unfortunately I too have been less strong and able during the last two years, so that life is a distressing problem.

Though still in her early fifties, Alice had aged considerably since leaving Yucatan.

Even the Le Plongeons had to concede that they would never see Yucatan again.

Augustus Le Plongeon died in Brooklyn on December 13, 1908, at the age of eighty-two. A few close friends attended the funeral, and he was cremated at Fresh Pond the next day. Alice scattered the ashes of her beloved Augustus at sea.

The *Brooklyn Eagle* published an obituary mentioning his early work on religion done while in Peru, as well as his more recent and better known fieldwork.

In addition to his interesting works on the discoveries he made in Yucatan, and which, it is said, aroused jealousies and disagreements in other archaeologists, Dr. Le Plongeon wrote many books in Spanish dealing with religion.

Mrs. Le Plongeon is in possession of many manuscripts by the doctor which have not yet been published. Among the most interesting of these, is a work called "Pearls in Shells," which is a frank and somewhat daring treatise on religions.

⊓ ⊓ ⊓

Alice's last major published work, *A Dream of Atlantis,* appeared serially from 1909 to 1911 in four volumes of the Theosophical Society's *The Word* magazine. She began her lengthy fictional account of Maya kingdoms by crediting Augustus's many years of study with giving her the understanding to write the present work. Her premise was that the "very ancient Mayas had, in remote times, gone forth from the west to people Atlantis, the same land which is called Mu in the Troano Manuscript according to the translation of Le Plongeon."

Alice wanted the reader to be aware that Augustus had interpreted many Maya manuscripts including the ancient Codex Troano, a fragment of one of the few authentic Maya books, which had been reprinted a few years earlier by Brasseur de Bourbourg.[1]

Alice's interpretations evolved out of her husband's, which as much as stated that the Maya founded Atlantis. Augustus saw the Maya as the source of all world civilization, and the greatest bearers of culture to the ancient world. Alice's *Dream of Atlantis* brought the Maya back to Yucatan from Atlantis.

> A few years prior to the destruction of that famous land a colony of the Old Maya stock again returned to the fatherland, in these days named Yucatan, and there founded a new empire that was under the rule of the Cans, the first king of this dynasty having been unanimously proclaimed by the colonists as their chosen monarch.

Battles and epic events marched across the pages of *The Word* for the next three years.

In the spring of 1910 Alice traveled to London to visit her family and draw up her will. Through her trusted friend Mrs. Henry Field (Maude) Blackwell, she planned for publication to continue even after her own death, which she felt could not be far off. Alice's will directed that all the Le Plongeons' manuscripts, notes, artifacts, and the hundreds of glass-plate negatives should be left in the care of Maude Blackwell.

Before leaving London she published "The Mystery of Egypt: Whence Came Her Ancestors?" in *The London Magazine*. She then set sail for New York, but during the crossing she became seriously ill. A friend of the Le Plongeons, Colonel James Churchward, had planned to meet Alice's ship. But other business interfered, and not realizing the gravity of her condition, he called upon Herbert Spinden, assistant curator of anthropology at the Natural History Museum, to assist Alice.

Alice was taken to New York's Woman's Hospital, where she survived for three weeks. Her friend Maude Blackwell came to her bedside to receive Alice's final instructions. Alice spoke of the frustration she and Augustus felt in seeing how their life's work was misunderstood and ignored. She gave their manuscripts and other materials to Mrs. Blackwell, asking her to guard them until the American people evinced a greater interest in the ancient Maya civilization than they had done in her lifetime and that of her husband. Blackwell promised to see Augustus's last major work, "The Origins of the Egyptians," into press with the Theosophical Publishing Company.

Alice Dixon Le Plongeon died on June 8, 1910. Obituaries in the *New York Times* and *New York Evening Post* called her "a writer of note" and a lecturer on "Central American subjects." Alice's death brought to a close more than half a century of fieldwork, writing, and lecturing by the Le Plongeons; but it did not end their influence on American archaeology. The mysteries of the Maya, which they felt had begun to be revealed to them—or perhaps had welled up from within their subconscious—would be left for others to unravel.

Epilogue

In judging of the subject here presented, the reader will bear in mind that facts substantiated should not be rejected, even if the theories founded on them advance beyond the light of present information.—Stephen Salisbury in "Dr. Le Plongeon in Yucatan," (1877:108)

After Augustus Le Plongeon's death it was difficult to be lukewarm about him. He was loved by close friends and intimates, but thoroughly ridiculed by those who disagreed with him. His articles on diffusion and his books, especially *Queen Móo and the Egyptian Sphinx,* provided the fuel for posthumous attacks on his work, and sometimes on his character as well, by those who did not share his views.

In a 1909 book on New World civilizations, Channing Arnold and Frederick Frost labeled Le Plongeon's ideas on Maya diffusion as "the most remarkable of all theories." Though giving him credit for being brave and having the "genius of enthusiasm," they ridiculed his work saying, "he dated the civilization of Central America 11,500 years back. This preposterous proposition was received with the Homeric laughter it so richly deserves."[1]

With Augustus's work being given this kind of reception it was no wonder that Maude Blackwell rejected an offer from Frederick Putnam of the Peabody Museum at Harvard to purchase the Chichen Itza mural tracings and other materials for the museum. It was only a short while since Alice had given her deathbed instructions to wait until such time that the American people showed a serious interest in Maya civilization. If she saw no sign of such interest as her life neared its end, Maude Blackwell was determined to personally destroy everything, following her friends' requests.

Instead she worked diligently at perpetuating their memory. She oversaw publication of the culmination of Augustus's lifework, "The Origins of the Egyptians." *The Word* published it serially throughout 1913 and 1914. In it Augustus traced the Maya through India, the Middle East, and Egypt, where he said they founded settlements as they went.

Augustus's reputation continued to be harmed by the persistent rumors of his use of dynamite. Ironically, as the untrue story grew and changed, the supposed use changed from Uxmal to Chichen Itza and became entwined with their excavation of the platforms. It may have been a passing reference by Le Plongeon's contemporary Teobert Maler, who arrived in Yucatan in 1884, that became the basis for the shift in location. Eduard Seler, who also worked at Chichen Itza and Uxmal, decried Le Plongeon's archaeological destruction of the platform mounds. The dynamite story in one form or another continued to feed on itself and is today one of the most persistent misunderstandings about Le Plongeon.

There were some writers, however, many of whom wrote for the popular press, who were still sympathetic to Le Plongeon's ideas. In a 1912 *American Antiquarian and Oriental Journal* article, John O. Viking backed Le Plongeon's statement that Christ's last words on the cross were spoken in Maya. Willis Fletcher Johnson, writing about "Pioneers of Mayan Research" for *The Outlook* in 1923, was also sympathetic to Le Plongeon's diffusionist ideas. He decried the injustices inflicted upon him by the academic community.

> Some of the most influential leaders and patrons of American archaeological and ethnological research apparently set themselves to discredit Dr. Le Plongeon and to prevent recognition of his achievements. They derided him and denounced him as a romancer and fabricator.

On the other hand, Lewis Spence, the latest in a long line of writers trying to prove the existence of Atlantis, attacked Le Plongeon's work in a 1924 book called *The Problem of Atlantis*. "We must absolutely cast behind us the wild and unscientific theories and alleged 'discoveries' of Le Plongeon and his school."

Theodore Willard, an industrialist and Maya enthusiast, wrote a popular book about Chichen Itza, called *The City of the Sacred Well*. In it he quoted at length Edward H. Thompson, who owned the Hacienda Chichen for many years and extensively explored the ruins. Thompson recognized the Le Plongeons' herculean efforts in the field and noted that Maya excavators who had worked on the Platform of Venus excavation called Augustus "a very positive man." "And from all his years of labor," Thompson told Willard, "Dr. Le Plongeon evolved a Mayan theology which is either inspired or the result of a mentality unhinged by too great labor."

James Churchward, a longtime friend of Alice and Augustus, acknowledged the influence of Augustus on his book, *The Lost Continent of Mu*. "Before the death of Dr. Le Plongeon he gave the writer his unpublished notes and translations for copy; so that what I say comes principally from the result of Dr. Le Plongeon's twelve years among the ruins." Churchward credited Le Plongeon with a number of insights pertaining to the theory that the continent of Mu, Churchward's Atlantis of the Pacific, was responsible for world civilization.

No doubt the support for Le Plongeon by individuals like Churchward, who himself was highly controversial, merely served to further emphasize the questionable parts of Le Plongeon's work.

In 1927 Augustus and Alice's contributions to archaeology were discussed in a series of letters to the editor of the *New York Times*. A devotee of Chinese literature, Alexander McAllen, claimed that a Chinese book explained the significance of the Chacmool figure. He praised Le Plongeon for grasping the importance of the statue without the aid of the book. As have many others commenting on Le Plongeon's work, he molded the Old Doctor's conclusions to his own designs.

In response, John Opdycke, an old acquaintance of the Le Plongeons', praised McAllan for helping point out that the then current writers on the Maya such as Otis Mason and Spinden, who were receiving so much attention, were not the true trailblazers on ancient Mexico.

> No matter what degree of difference there may be
> between the more recent students of Mayan
> archaeology and the Le Plongeons, there can be no
> doubt that the modern school has been indifferent,
> not to say professionally discourteous to these good

people, who were the first really great experts in regard to the ancient Mayan peoples.

Opdycke alluded to their love of humanity.

> The Le Plongeons were scientists not only, but they were, as well, artists and philosophers in the field of archaeology. They touched nothing with the hand of scientific research that they were not able to adorn with rational, albeit, artistic, interpretation.

Professional journals, when they mentioned Le Plongeon's work at all, were less flattering. Herbert J. Spinden, at that time a widely regarded Mayanist of the Peabody Museum at Harvard University, placed Le Plongeon with "the most daring group of romantic writers" in anthropology, accusing Le Plongeon of believing that the Maya crossed Atlantis "to walk dry shod to Africa for the purpose of founding Egypt." Later in his *Maya Art and Civilization,* Spinden characterized references in Le Plongeon's writings as valuable, but found his theories and conclusions untenable.

That Augustus and Alice Le Plongeon's work continued to receive occasional positive notice was encouraging to Maude Blackwell. But she needed a different sort of sign to be convinced of the American people's readiness to accept the evidence about the Maya. She was waiting for something dramatic. It came in 1929. The *New York Times* published an aerial photograph of Chichen Itza taken while archaeologist Alfred Kidder flew over the ruined city with Charles Lindbergh. Maude Blackwell took this as the moment she was waiting for. She contacted the well-known archaeologist Sylvanus Morley, director of the Carnegie Institution's Chichen Itza project, and Frans Blom, director of Tulane University's Middle American Research Institute to inform them that she had the Le Plongeon materials.

Morley was astonished to learn that, contrary to the rumor that had spread among Mayanists, the Le Plongeon material still existed. He had been told by Alfred Tozzer, his professor of archaeology at Harvard University twenty-six years earlier, "that Dr. Le Plongeon had decided to burn all his notes and photographs just before his death to prevent their falling into the hands of such an ungrateful world" (Morley 1931). He and Karl Ruppert, also a Carnegie archaeologist, arranged to meet Blackwell in Los Angeles where she had taken the materials.

Meanwhile Blom wrote back to Blackwell, "I would like to see these papers, not only for the valuable material they may contain, but also because I should like to incorporate them in our library." She sent him another letter with a few photos and some plans of structures at Chichen Itza and Uxmal.

Apparently the meeting with Morley and Ruppert did not go well. As Blackwell described it in a second letter to Frans Blom,

> Of course I ought to have been prepared to find that the two archaeologists are *too conservative* to pay much attention to Dr. Le Plongeon's theories, etc. In more ways than one I was disappointed in their visit here. TIME will prove as to which set of 'theories' lies nearest the truth.

Morley had problems relating to Blackwell as well. He wrote to the Carnegie Institution, "I spent from noon to ten o'clock one night trying to get concrete facts from her and to pin her down to anything." As a result Blackwell broke off negotiations with Morley. In contrast Blom seemed much more interested and sincere, but acquisition was hampered by the distance between Los Angeles and New Orleans.

Concurrent with the negotiations with Morley and Blom, Blackwell had also contacted Manly P. Hall, president of the Philosophical Research Society, a private research and educational institution in Los Angeles. She found Hall to be a more sympathetic individual. His sincere interest in the Le Plongeons' work convinced Blackwell to sell their materials to the Philosophical Research Society in 1931. The collection of several hundred photographs, glass-plate negatives, tracings of Maya murals, and memorabilia remains there today.

In her discussions with Blom, Morley, Ruppert, and Hall, Blackwell suggested that Alice's deathbed statements disclosed that the Le Plongeons had uncovered a number of Maya codices in Yucatan during their years of fieldwork. If true this would have been a major discovery, since only three hieroglyphic texts were known to have survived. Any new codices found would be of immense help to Maya research and would bring great fame to the finder.

With the best of intentions, Blackwell had attempted to right the reputation of Augustus Le Plongeon. She may have hoped that the hints and confused statements she attributed to Alice and Augustus might lead an archaeologist to stumble onto a cache of codices, thereby indirectly giving credit to the Le Plongeons. Her attempt merely magnified the confusion about their lives and work. Shortly after leaving the Le Plongeon materials with Manly Hall, Blackwell left Los Angeles and returned to her home in New York. The possibilities left by the Le Plongeon legacy dangled tantalizingly. Various individuals, including some Maya archaeologists who chose not to admit they believed the tale, may have quietly looked for a trace of Augustus's codices.

In 1940 archaeologist Harry E. D. Pollock mentioned Augustus Le Plongeon in "Sources and Methods in the Study of Maya Architecture." He credited Augustus with being "the first to perform any considerable amount of excavation" in the Maya area, and pointed out the importance of "the new material that appeared in his photographs, plans and drawings." However, he added, "his lurid imagination made his writing almost valueless."

Manly Hall also noted the importance of the Le Plongeons' photographs to the study of Maya civilization in "The Maya Empire," a 1948 article published in the Philosophical Research Society's magazine, *Horizon*. Perhaps for the first time, a scholar was looking at the Le Plongeons' work in the context of the nineteenth century to attempt a fair estimation of their contribution to Maya archaeology.

> Le Plongeon could not censor his discoveries by referring to the learned texts of other authors. He did not have the benefit of the works of the great institutions, which have since spent millions of dollars and sent dozens of experts to examine the field. He and his wife could report only what they actually found, but it was impossible for them to be in the presence of so many wonders without doing a little wondering themselves.

Hall found it interesting that many in the scientific world had formed opinions on Maya archaeology without the benefit of practical experience: "With the caution natural to their kind, these savants questioned, criticized, and condemned all of Le Plongeon's findings."

Few took note of Hall's observations; and with the deaths of Morley and others involved in the abortive attempts to acquire Le Plongeon's photographs, their whereabouts were largely forgotten. One scholar who did look at them briefly was Professor H. B. Nicholson, an archaeologist and ethnohistorian at UCLA. He found them intriguing, but set any work on them aside in favor of other, more pressing, projects.

In the mid-1950s, a trunk belonging to Maude Blackwell was delivered to archaeologist William Duncan Strong of Columbia University in New York. It arrived unannounced from a storage company, when storage payments stopped, presumably upon Blackwell's death. It contained some of her personal possessions, as well as some negatives, prints, and lantern slides of Augustus Le Plongeon's. Strong sent the trunk and its contents to Gordon Ekholm, curator of anthropology for the American Museum of Natural History in New York since it seemed of more interest to a museum.

These were the last fragments of Le Plongeon research materials to come to light. No hoped-for archaeological field notes or diaries from their years in Yucatan or unpublished manuscripts, such as the "Pearls in Shells" treatise on religion, have been found. Perhaps in the attic of an old home in New York or London sits a trunk full of the missing photographs, field notes, and manuscripts.

In 1962, a popular book by archaeologist Robert Wauchope, *Lost Tribes and Sunken Continents,* devoted a chapter to Augustus Le Plongeon. It was highly critical of every aspect of his work. According to Wauchope, Le Plongeon's "arrogant flaunting of his own ego produced a lurid epoch in the history of American archaeology."

A decade later historian Robert Brunhouse wrote *In Search of the Maya,* a book on eight early archaeologists. In it he gave a somewhat more balanced account of Augustus Le Plongeon. Alice's activities were noted; however, her contribution was minimized by the suggestion that her husband was the source of all her ideas. And Augustus was summarized as "mysterious, preposterous, opinionated, haphazardly informed, reckless, and a remarkable figure."

Recent writers on Maya history and American archaeology have distilled Le Plongeon to one sentence throwaways. He has been called many things, including "one of the most fantastic characters in American archaeology" (Willey and Sabloff 1974:65), a "French antiquarian and mystic" (Gallencamp 1985:32), and a "master of self-deception" (Miller 1985:7).

For many years, Maude Blackwell's statements about codices found by the Le Plongeons remained a mystery, since efforts to locate possible hiding places had proved fruitless. However, recent research on Augustus Le Plongeon's life brought to light a letter he wrote in 1907 to Charles P. Bowditch, patron of the Peabody Museum at Harvard, revealing that he had never unearthed any codices. Bowditch was interested in Le Plongeon's interpretations of Maya hieroglyphics and iconography, and attempted to get Augustus to divulge where he thought Maya codices might be hidden. In reply to one inquiry from Bowdich, Augustus explained that he had no codices hidden away in Yucatan.

> [I] may be induced perhaps, to mention some of the places where such records may still exist and where some years ago, I began to look, when my researches were interrupted by events beyond my control. I have no objection to tell you that, in my

own mind, I am convinced that very ancient Mss.
exist at Chichen. . . . If I had money of my own I
would be willing to spend it to bring to light these
ancient books.

These were brave and proud words from an old man who
lay near death, but who nevertheless refused to give up his
dream of revealing the true history of the Maya.

ᒋ ᒋ ᒋ

Was Augustus Le Plongeon really a crackpot? The question will persist, no doubt. He came into Maya studies as a
renaissance man unencumbered by geographic or discipli-
nary boundaries which were being formed at the time. He
chose to ignore them if they did not fit his need or world
view. His experiences around the world and with various
professions told him that a little research and experimentation could perfect any process. It worked in his surveying
and photographic careers. He met little or no opposition to
his experiments and writings on earthquakes and "electro-
hydropathic" medicine. He tried to apply this principle to
the study of world civilizations with less success.

In contrast, Alice Le Plongeon arrived in Yucatan as a
young woman, seeing the world for the first time. As one
of the first European women to carry out research in that
area, she had to make her own rules as she went. She quickly
learned the skills she needed to be her husband's partner
in their work. And on her own she made significant contributions to the understanding of the social history and
living conditions of the Maya.

It is clear that the Le Plongeons made a worthwhile
contribution to American archaeology with their photographic documentation, descriptions, and drawings. And
their outdated theories provide us with a perspective into
the developing field of archaeology during the nineteenth
century. They carried the validation of the worth of New
World civilization to an extreme that even the strongest
proponents of New World studies could not accept. Augustus
Le Plongeon promoted worldwide diffusion of Maya culture
at a time when opposition to diffusion from either direction
was beginning to gather scholarly momentum. He had made
his case through comparative religion and linguistics, but
the new level of scholarship all but demolished his arguments. Daniel Brinton, and later scholars and field archaeologists such as Eduard Seler, Alfred Maudslay, and Sylvanus
Morley found virtually no basis for such a position.

Ironically what Augustus considered to be his greatest

find, the Chacmool statue from Chichen Itza, may have been his worst enemy. It confirmed to him that the Maya were the founders of Egyptian civilization. Had he not found the statue, he might have given up that particular line of reasoning. But undaunted he fought on until his death and suffered complete rejection by the very scholars whom he considered to be lesser intellects.

Notes

Chapter 4

1. Current interpretations of this inscription suggest that it records the accession to kingship.

2. His plan is accurate to within a few centimeters of current plans of the structure.

3. Those bas-reliefs have become severely eroded by weather and pollution in the last one hundred years.

4. Today the murals are variously interpreted as mythical, mildly historical, or related to astronomical phenomena.

Chapter 6

1. Archaeologists are still puzzled by these small buildings, which were probably for ritual purposes.

2. Chan Santa Cruz was later to become Felipe Carillo Puerto after the Maya's defeat in 1910.

Chapter 8

1. After reading Le Plongeon's article on Mayapan, Archaeoastronomer Anthony Aveni found that Augustus had a "deep knowledge of astronomy and navigation," but regarded as "lacking any evidence" his rather tortuous attempt to credit the Maya with knowledge of the use of the gnomon for keeping time. Archaeologists have never relocated the gnomon mound.

Chapter 9

1. The most common explanation of this phenomenon in Maya architecture is the need for heavy walls to support the monumental stone ceilings associated with corbelled arches.

Chapter 11

1. Now called the Platform of Venus because of the Venus glyphs in relief on its sides.
2. The cones can still be seen at Chichen Itza. They have distinct tonal qualities when struck, which has recently led some archaeologists to speculate that they might have been used as stone drums.
3. An extension of this floor to the north was seen in 1981 by Lawrence Desmond in a trench dug for electrical cables to be used in the Sound-and-Light Show.
4. Art historians have found the face and beard to represent ethnic peoples of Mexico and Yucatan.

Chapter 14

1. Bourbourg's work on the Troano, now called the Madrid Codex, was superficial, and dealt only with selected parts.

Bibliography

Athenaeum
  1896   A review of *Queen Móo and the Egyptian Sphinx*,
           August 29:296.

Aveni, Anthony
  1984   Colgate University, Hamilton, New York. Personal
           communication, November 30.

Arnold, Channing and Frederick J. Frost
  1909   *The American Egypt*. Double Day, Page, New York.

Aymé, Louis
  1880   Letter to Stephen Salisbury, Jr., December 1. Amer-
           ican Antiquarian Society, Worcester.

Betts, Brooks
  1911   *The Fall of Maya, A Tragic Drama of Ancient Amer-*
           ica. In 5 acts and 10 scenes, with an introduction
           and epilogue. Undated review in ms. folder. New
           York Public Library, New York.

Blackwell, Maude
1931   Letter to Frans Blom, November 16. Tulane University, Latin American Library.

Blavatsky, Helena P.
1888   *The Secret Doctrine.* (2 volumes) The Theosophical Publishing Company, Ltd., London.

Blom, Frans
1931   Letter to Maude Blackwell, July 22. Tulane University, Latin American Library.

Bourbourg, Brasseur de
1857–59 *Histoire des nations civilisées du Mexique et de l'Amérique centrale.* N.p., Paris.
1868   *Quatre lettres sur le Mexique.* Maisonneuve et Co., Paris.

Brinton, Daniel
1885   Notes on American Ethnology. *The American Antiquarian and Oriental Journal* VIII (6):378.
1890   *Essays of an Americanist.* Porter and Coates, Philadelphia.

California Academy of Sciences
1873   *Proceedings of the California Academy of Sciences* 1868–1872 (Vol. IV), December. San Francisco.

Carillo y Ancona, Crescencio
1886   *Los Cabezas-Chatas.* Anales del Museo Nacional (Tomo III), pp. 272–78. Imprenta de Ignacio Escalante, Mexico.

Charnay, Désiré
1887   *Ancient Cities of the New World.* Harper and Brothers, New York.

Churchward, James
1926   *The Lost Continent of Mu.* William E. Rudge, New York.

Cirerol Sansores, Manuel
1957   *Chi cheen Itza.* Talleres Graficas del sudeste, Yucatan.

Davis, Keith
1981   *Désiré Charnay: Expeditionary Photographer.* University of New Mexico Press, Albuquerque.

Darwin, Charles
1871   *The Descent of Man and Selection in Relation to Sex.* Vol. II. John Murray, London.

Desmond, Lawrence G.
1983   *Augustus Le Plongeon: Early Maya Archaeologist.* Unpublished Ph.D. dissertation, University of Colorado, Boulder.

Gallenkamp, Charles and Regina E. Johnson, eds.
1985   *Maya: Treasures of an Ancient Civilization.* Abrams, New York.

Hall, Manly P.
1948   The Maya Empire. With special reference to the work of Augustus Le Plongeon. *Horizon* 7 (4):23–35.

Haven, Samuel F.
  1856   *Archaeology of the United States*. Smithsonian Contributions to Knowledge, 8.
  1877   Report to the librarian. *Proceedings of the American Antiquarian Society,* 70:89–100.

Hubbard, Elbert
  1897   Review of *Queen Móo and the Egyptian Sphinx. The Arena* 17:342–45.

Johnson, Willis F.
  1923   Pioneers of Mayan Research. *The Outlook* 134:474–76.

Landa, Diego De
  1941   *Relación de las Cosas de Yucatán*. A translation, Alfred M. Tozzer, ed., Papers of the Peabody Museum, 18, Cambridge.

L'Echo du Pacific
  1856   Advertisement for Augustus Le Plongeon's photographic studio. May 21:4, San Francisco.

Le Plongeon, Alice
  1877   Letter to Mrs. Gaylord, April 3. American Antiquarian Society.
  1879   Notes on Yucatan. *Proceedings of the American Antiquarian Society* 72:77–106.
  1881a   Ruined Uxmal. *The New York World,* June 27:1–2.
  1881b   Ruined Uxmal. *The New York World,* July 18:2.
  1881c   Yucatan's Buried Cities. *The New York World,* November 27:10.
  1884a   Dr. Le Plongeon's Latest and Most Important Discoveries among the Ruined Cities of Yucatan. *Scientific American,* Supplement 448, August 3:7143–47.
  1884b   Plague of Locusts in Yucatan. *Scientific American,* Supplement 449, August 9:7174.
  1885   The New and Old in Yucatan. *Harper's Magazine* 70:372–86.
  1886a   *Here and There in Yucatan*. J. W. Bouton, New York.
  1886b   Yucatan, Its Ancient Temples and Palaces (abstract). *New York Academy of Sciences Transactions* V:169–78.
  1887a   The Mayas: Their Customs, Laws and Religion. *Magazine of American History* 17:233–38.
  1887b   Eastern Yucatan, its Scenery, People, and Ancient Cities and Monuments (abstract). *New York Academy of Sciences Transactions* (November 7) VII:45–48.
  1888   The Conquest of the Mayas. *Magazine of American History* 20:115–20.
  1890   The Mayas. *Theosophical Siftings,* Vol. 3, No. 14. Theosophical Publishing Society, London.
  1894   Early Architecture and Engineering in Peru. *The Engineering Magazine* 7 (1):46–60.

1896? Letter to Phoebe A. Hearst, undated. Bancroft Library, Berkeley.

1900a Letter to Phoebe A. Hearst, March 17. Bancroft Library, Berkeley.

1900b Letter to Phoebe A. Hearst, March 18. Bancroft Library, Berkeley.

1902 *Queen Móo's Talisman*. Peter Eckler Publisher, New York.

1905 Letter to Phoebe A. Hearst, March 4. Bancroft Library, Berkeley.

1909a Augustus Le Plongeon, M.D., L.L.D. *Journal de Societe des Americanistes* (Paris), No. 2:176–279.

1909–11 A Dream of Atlantis. *The Word Magazine* IX, X, XI, XII. The Theosophical Publishing Company, New York.

1910 The Mystery of Egypt: Whence Came her Ancestors? The *London Magazine* 24 (140):121–32.

Le Plongeon, Augustus

1867 *La religion de Jesus comparada con las enseñanzas de la Iglesia*. W. White and Co., Boston.

1869 *Los Jesuitas e el Peru*. W. White and Co., Boston.

1872 The Causes of Earthquakes. *Van Nostrand's Eclectric Engineering Magazine* 6:537–44, 557–84.

1873a Vestiges of Antiquity. An address to the Geographical Society of New York. Published in part in the *New York Tribune* Lecture and Letter Extras, No. 8.

1873b *Manual de fotografía*. Scovill Manufacturing Company, New York.

1876 Letter to Chas. F. Meudue, December 12. American Antiquarian Society, Worcester.

1877a Letter to General Protasio Guerra, February 21. American Antiquarian Society, Worcester.

1877b Letter to Stephen Salisbury, Jr., September 1. American Antiquarian Society, Worcester.

1878a Letter to Stephen Salisbury, Jr., February 19. American Antiquarian Society, Worcester.

1878b Letter to Stephen Salisbury, Jr., May 13. American Antiquarian Society, Worcester.

1879 Archaeological Communication on Yucatan. *Proceedings of the American Antiquarian Society*, 72:65–75.

1880a Letter to Stephen Salisbury, Jr., September 29. American Antiquarian Society, Worcester.

1880b Letter to Stephen Salisbury, Jr., November 2. American Antiquarian Society, Worcester.

1880c An open letter from Professor Le Plongeon, of Belize, British Honduras. *The Present Century* 2:337–39.

1881a *Vestiges of the Mayas*. J. Polhemus, New York.

1881b Mayapan and Maya Inscriptions. *Proceedings of the American Antiquarian Society* (New Series) 1:246–82.

1881c   Letter to Stephen Salisbury, Jr., July 30. American Antiquarian Society, Worcester.

1881d   An Interesting Discovery. A Temple with Masonic Symbols in the Ruined City of Uxmal. *Harpers Weekly,* December 17:851–52.

1882a   Letter to Stephen Salisbury, Jr., June 8. American Antiquarian Society, Worcester.

1882b   Letter to George F. Hoar, June 24. Peabody Museum, Harvard.

1886   *Sacred Mysteries among the Mayas and Quiches, 11,500 Years Ago.* Macoy Publishing, New York.

1889   Letter to Stephen Salisbury, Jr., January 7. American Antiquarian Society, Worcester.

1896   *Queen Móo and the Egyptian Sphinx.* By the author, New York.

1902   Letter to William J. McGee, August 15. Smithsonian Institution, Washington, D.C.

1907   Letter to Charles Bowditch, May 28. The Peabody Museum, Harvard.

1913–14   The Origin of the Egyptians. *The Word Magazine* Vols. 17 and 18.

Lespinasse, A. J.
1877   Letter to Augustus Le Plongeon, March 8. American Antiquarian Society, Worcester.

Mayer, Brantz
1857   Observations on Mexican History and Archaeology, with a Special Notice of Zapotec Remains. Smithsonian Contributions to Knowledge, 9.

McAllen, Alexander
1927   Old Chinese Records Tell of Maya's "Sudden Sickness." *New York Times,* February 20:(7):18

McElroy, Keith
1977   *The History of Photography in Peru in the Nineteenth Century: 1839–1876.* Unpublished Ph.D. dissertation, University of New Mexico, Albuquerque.

Miller, Mary E.
1985   A Re-examination of the Mesoamerican Chacmool. *Art Bulletin* 67(1):7–17.

Morley, Sylvanus
1931   Letter to J. C. Merriam, October 10. Carnegie Institution, Washington, D.C.

The Nation [New York]
1878   Notes, 27 (684):84.
1879   Sources of Spanish-American History, 28 (720):265.

New York Evening Mail
1871   Art Gossip. Three important paintings from Peru. March 2:1.

New York Evening Post
1910   Obituary of Alice Dixon Le Plongeon. June 9.

New York Times

1887   Sketches of Yucatan. A review of *Here and There in Yucatan,* May 29:14.

1910   Obituary of Alice Dixon Le Plongeon. June 10:9.

Ober, Frederick A.

1884   *Travels in Mexico.* J. Dewing and Company, Boston.

Opdycke, John

1927   Le Plongeon's Mayan Research. *New York Times,* February 27:(8):14.

Periódico Oficial

1877   The Statue of Chacmol. Merida, Yucatan, March 2.

Pollock, H. E. D.

1940   Sources and Methods in the Study of Maya Architecture. In *The Maya and their Neighbors,* Cooper Square Publishers, New York, new edition 1973.

Putnam, Frederick W.

1902   Memorandum to President Jesup, March 25. American Museum of Natural History, New York.

1911   Letter to Mrs. Henry Field (Maude) Blackwell, January 26. American Museum of Natural History, New York.

Ramey, Earl

1966   *Augustus Le Plongeon.* Address to the Mary Aaron Museum Society, April 12. John Packard Library, Marysville, California.

Reed, Nelson

1964   *The Caste War of Yucatan.* Stanford University Press.

Salisbury, Stephen, Jr.

1877   Dr. Le Plongeon in Yucatan. *Proceedings of the American Antiquarian Society* 69:70–119.

1878   Terra Cotta Figure from Isla Mujeres. *Proceedings of the American Antiquarian Society* 71–89.

San Francisco Daily Evening Bulletin

1855   Advertisement for Augustus Le Plongeon's photographic studio, August 20.

Scientific American

1895   A Woman Archaeologist. Supplement 1023, August 10:83.

Seler, Eduard

1915   *Amerikanische Altertumskunde* Vol. 5. Behrend and Company, Berlin.

Spence, Lewis

1924   *The Problem of Atlantis.* Brentano's New York.

Spinden, Herbert J.

1927   The Prosaic vs. the Romantic School in Anthropology. In *Culture: The Diffusion Controversy,* W. W. Norton and Company, New York.

Squier, Ephraim G. and Edwin H. Davis

1848   *Ancient Monuments of the Mississippi Valley.* Smithsonian Contributions to Knowledge, No. 1, Washington, D.C.

Stephens, John L.
    1843   *Incidents of Travel in Yucatan*. Harper and Brothers,
        New York.

Tax, Thomas G.
    1973   *The Development of American Archaeology: 1800–*
        1879. Unpublished Ph.D. dissertation, University of
        Chicago.

Thompson, Charles O.
    1880   Letter to Stephen Salisbury, Jr. American Antiquar-
        ian Society, Worcester.

Thompson, Edward H.
    1931   A Maya Legend in the Making. *Proceedings of the*
        American Antiquarian Society 61:340–43.

Valentini, Philipp J. J.
    1882   The Olmecas and the Tultecas: A Study in Early
        Mexican Ethnology and History. *Proceedings of the*
        American Antiquarian Society (New Series) II:193–
        230.

Viking, John O.
    1912   The Petrified Clam; or Eli, Eli, Lamah Sabachtani.
        The American Antiquarian and Oriental Journal 34
        (3):190–92.

Wake, C. Stanisland
    1904   The Mayas of Central America. *The American Anti-*
        quarian and Oriental Journal 26:361–63.

Wauchope, Robert
    1962   *Lost Tribes and Sunken Continents*. University of
        Chicago Press.

Willard, Theodore
    1926   *The City of the Sacred Well*. New York Century
        Company.

Willey, Gordon R. and Jeremy A. Sabloff
    1974   *A History of American Archaeology*. W. H. Freeman
        and Company, San Francisco.

Index

file, 65–66; story of royal family recreated, 103

Valentini, Philipp J., 61, 85, 87
Vestiges of the Mayas, 39
Volan coche, 19

Wake, C. S., review of *Queen Móo,* 119–20
Waldeck, Jean Fredérick, work in Maya area, xx

War of the Castes, 16, 17. *See also* Canek, Jacinto; Chan Santa Cruz Maya

Yucatan Peninsula: 15, 46–47; Le Plongeons' arrival, 15; Ecab, 46–47; Aluxob; Niscute, small buildings, 47

Zoc, consort of Canchi, 103